From the Editor's Desk

*Thinking Critically, Living Faithfully
at the Dawn of a New Christian Century*

John M. Buchanan

With Chapter Introductions
by Jason Byassee

WESTMINSTER
JOHN KNOX PRESS
LOUISVILLE · KENTUCKY

First edition
Published by Westminster John Knox Press
Louisville, Kentucky

16 17 18 19 20 21 22 23 24 25—10 9 8 7 6 5 4 3 2 1

Book design by Drew Stevens and Ann V. DeVilbiss
Cover design by Allison Taylor
Cover photograph: Daniel Richardson. Used by permission.

Library of Congress Cataloging-in-Publication Data

Names: Buchanan, John M., 1938– author.
Title: From the editor's desk : thinking critically, living faithfully at the dawn of a
  new Christian century / John Buchanan, with Jason Byassee.
Other titles: Christian century (Chicago, Ill. : 1902)
Description: First edition. | Louisville, KY : Westminster John Knox Press, 2016. |
  Editorials reprinted from Christian century.
Identifiers: LCCN 2016018917 (print) | LCCN 2016030762 (ebook) | ISBN
  9780664261252 (pbk. : alk. paper) | ISBN 9781611647785 (ebk.)
Subjects: LCSH: Christianity. | Editorials.
Classification: LCC BR124 .B83 2016 (print) | LCC BR124 (ebook) | DDC
  270.8/3--dc23
LC record available at https://lccn.loc.gov/2016018917

♾ The paper used in this publication meets the minimum requirements of the American National Standard for Information Sciences—Permanence of Paper for Printed Library Materials, ANSI Z39.48-1992.

Contents

Introduction

THE *CHRISTIAN CENTURY*: PAST, PRESENT, AND FUTURE

It must have been an extraordinary time to be alive in the 1890s as the nineteenth century gave way to the twentieth. Karen Armstrong nicely characterizes the beginning of the twentieth century in her book *The Case for God* by telling about the confident optimism, the cheerful buoyancy of the Second International Congress of Mathematicians that convened in Paris in 1900. German mathematician David Hilbert stood up and announced that there were just twenty-three outstanding problems in the Newtonian system, and once these twenty-three remaining puzzles were solved, we would pretty much know everything there is to know about the universe. Hilbert went on to predict a century of unparalleled scientific progress. Permanent peace and prosperity seemed to be within reach. There appeared to be no limit to what human beings could and would accomplish.

In June of 1910, a World Missionary Conference was convened in Edinburgh. Twelve hundred delegates from around the world gathered to talk about interchurch collaboration in the global missionary enterprise. The chairperson was John R. Mott. Among the distinguished delegates, all housed in Edinburgh homes, were Lord Balfour, the Archbishop of Canterbury, and William Jennings Bryan, who spoke eloquently about global education as part of the mission project. Bryan, years before his humiliation and tragic demise in a small Tennessee courtroom, was so good he combined a speaking tour of Scotland with his service at the conference. Also present was Robert E. Speer, one of the saints of American Presbyterianism; Tasuku Harada, the President of Doshisha University in Japan; Sherwood Eddy; and the Bishop of the Church of Sweden.

Taking it all in, as well, was a thirty-six-year-old American delegate, a minister in the Christian church, Disciples of Christ, Charles Clayton Morrison. Two years earlier he had purchased a floundering journal, the *Christian Century*, and as he put it, "refounded it." He wired back to Chicago an editorial, published on July 7, 1910, in which he described sitting in the drawing room of his host, taking tea (he was a teetotaler), and listening to his host describe the conference as "about the biggest thing that ever struck Scotland." In fact, Morrison reported that the Archbishop of Canterbury looked around at the assembly and observed, "If men be weighted rather than counted, this assemblage has, I suppose, no parallel in the history of this or other lands."

The conference identified sectarian division among Christians as the most formidable obstacle to the advancement of the Christian gospel globally. Hope and optimism ran high. Morrison wrote: "Everyone feels the presence of a power, not ourselves, deeper than our own devices, which is making for a triumphant advance of Christianity abroad . . . the delegates are thrilled by the sense that the conference foreshadows a new era for the church at home."

It is perhaps not possible for us to recapture the optimism and hope of the first decade of the twentieth century. Developments in physics, biology, and mathematics would make human life better, healthier, more free than it had ever been. Modern transport would bring the nations of the world closer to one another and, therefore, more inclined to be peaceful. Christianity, with a new vision of its power represented by ecumenism, reflected the general confidence by setting itself to the goal of actualizing the kingdom of God on earth—and the world for Christ in our time.

One of the later editors of Morrison's magazine wrote about that era:

> Protestants tiring of provincialism; churches breaking out of sectarian isolation. Scholars were beginning to speak the truth concerning history and the composition of the Bible, liberating some churches from literalism. Burgeoning industrialization had become so oppressive that the nation's conscience was hurting. Labor was stirring. Suffragettes were marching. Pioneer sociologists were uncovering the shame of city slums and the disgrace of child labor. Proposals to prohibit manufacture and sale of liquor were discussed and widely supported. The political arena was alive with humanitarian issues.[1]

The *Christian Century* was born at a time when thoughtful people believed that they were living at the beginning of it—the Christian century. The magazine was actually founded in 1884 as the Christian Oracle—a name someone quipped recently is actually worse than the *Christian Century*. It was a Disciples of Christ journal, which renamed itself the *Christian Century* in 1900, floundered, and was in mortgage foreclosure when Morrison bought it for $1,500 from a publishing broker in Chicago. He ran it as a for-profit corporation until his retirement in 1947.

His magazine became an eloquent voice for the social gospel. Wikipedia says we are "considered the flagship magazine of mainline Protestantism."[2] We describe ourselves this way: "For decades the *Christian Century* has informed and shaped progressive, mainline Christianity. Committed to thinking critically and living faithfully, the magazine explores what it means to believe and live out the Christian faith in our time. As a voice of generous orthodoxy the *Century* is both loyal to the church and open to the world."

The voice of the *Christian Century* has been important enough in the culture of American religion that two other journals were founded in disagreement with us: *Christianity and Crisis* and *Christianity Today*. We have never been large—45,000 was the biggest our subscription list ever was. Mostly we have been in the mid-30,000s. But we have been read by academics and pastors, evangelicals who we have infuriated with our liberal positions, and liberals who we have enraged by our not being liberal enough. One president read us and reads us still, I believe—Jimmy Carter—as did the legendary longtime North Carolina Tar Heels basketball coach, the late Dean Smith. (My secret goal is to get the magazine in the hands of the Ricketts family, the new owners of the Chicago Cubs!)

Contributors over the years have included Karl Barth, Paul Tillich, Reinhold Niebuhr, Gerald Ford, Martin Luther King Jr., Nelson Rockefeller, Walter Reuther, Karl Menninger, Robert Kennedy—and Spiro Agnew (not on my watch).

The *Christian Century* reported on, analyzed, and advocated for the issues that have characterized the age and compelled the conscience of the churches. On the topic of war the *Christian Century*, in its early years, advocated political action to outlaw war, and Morrison, so prominent in the peace movement, was invited to Paris to witness the signing of an international treaty, during the 1920s, to abolish war. Unfortunately, it had no provision for enforcement. As war threatened again in the 1930s, Morrison, who was not quite a pacifist (he called himself a "pragmatic noninterventionist") wrote consistently and powerfully against war and preparation for war. Only after Pearl Harbor did he change his mind, and then only reluctantly. He called the Second World War an "unnecessary necessity."

This attitude on international conflict was the subject of increasing tension between Morrison and Reinhold Niebuhr, a contributing editor and one of the magazine's most important and popular writers. Niebuhr's Christian realism required resisting evil, by force if necessary. He became so irritated with Morrison's pragmatic noninterventionism that he broke with the magazine in February of 1941, removed his name from the masthead, and launched his own magazine, *Christianity and Crisis*. It took years for the breach to heal, but eventually it did and Niebuhr resumed writing for the *Christian Century*.

Niebuhr also disagreed with Morrison over Prohibition. Morrison was a teetotaler and an avid proponent of Prohibition. Niebuhr, with perhaps a truer sense of humanity, thought it was all a big mistake. On another occasion Morrison tried to organize a movement simply to discuss important issues without becoming political. Niebuhr called it "pure moonshine."

The magazine took up the cause of organized labor, child labor, universal suffrage, and Native American rights, and during the war it launched a crusade against the internment of Japanese Americans.

After the war, the *Christian Century*, with Kyle Haselden as editor, focused on civil rights, advocating for equal rights for all Americans. Martin Luther King Jr. was invited to be a contributing editor and submitted articles. When he wrote "A Letter from the Birmingham Jail" to white ministers in Birmingham who had asked him to have patience and not push so hard for change, he sent it to the *Christian Century*, which was first to publish it in its entirety. Dean Peerman, who graduated from Yale Divinity School in 1959, went to work for the *Christian Century* that year and edited that letter using his manual Olympia typewriter. Dean Peerman, who recently retired from the magazine, marched with Martin Marty at Selma, and they came home and wrote about it powerfully in the magazine. Dean eventually turned in his typewriter and reluctantly learned to use a computer.

The *Christian Century* has ventured out into the dangerous field of national politics on occasion, particularly with the resurgence of political conservatism in the Republican Party, which seemed to *Century* editors as unfortunate, unhelpful, and not consistent with the deepest Christian values and hopes. Editor Kyle Haselden felt compelled to express his criticism of the Republican presidential candidate's positions, which he did in an editorial titled "Goldwater, No." He retired shortly thereafter, and his successor, Alan Geyer, felt that he couldn't just let that hang out there. So he wrote the counterpoint: "Johnson,

Yes." As a result, the IRS revoked the magazine's tax-exempt status for several years, alerted by none other than Billy James Hargis of the Christian Anti-Communist Crusade.

All the while the *Christian Century* was a consistent voice for ecumenism, reflecting Morrison's 1910 experience in Edinburgh. He personally reported on the Federal Council of Churches and the magazine applauded, reported on, and supported the New National Council of Churches and the World Council of Churches.

When I assumed the editor's desk in 1999, the church was in a very different place. The decline of the mainline churches in North America is so studied, lamented, observed, and exegeted as almost to be a cliché. No one knows that more than this Presbyterian, who can remember the denomination making news when our stated clerk, Eugene Carson Blake, appeared on the cover of *TIME* magazine with Episcopal Bishop James Pike at the launch of what became the Consultation on Church Union.

Douglas John Hall calls the shift of the last few decades "the end of Christendom," and it surely is that. Hall also says it is the opportunity for the church to find itself.

Martin Marty traces the sidelining of the colonial big three as America has diversified and urges all of us in the mainline church not to abandon who we are and what we do best: build community, educate for human rights, and advocate for the environment, which is under assault.[3]

Phyllis Tickle uses the image of an every-five-hundred-year rummage sale in a way that is both encouraging and frightening. It is encouraging because the result is always something new and better and more faithful, a reconstituted form of the church that is now leaner, more viable, and more faithful. And, says Tickle, the faith always spreads dramatically during such periods. But it's frightening if you worry or suspect that your traditions and practices might be among the items pulled out of the attic and unceremoniously dumped.[4]

The *Christian Century*'s response to this new place in which we find ourselves has been to invest a little more energy and attention in congregations where Christian faith is taught and nurtured and where discipleship is shaped and formed and where pastors lead. My hope is that the *Christian Century* will continue to be an irreplaceable resource to congregations struggling to be faithful, sometimes against very difficult odds and pastors who lead and who must stand up before congregations every week, in these daunting times, and say something faithful and useful. And to do that without losing the prophetic edginess, the thoughtful cultural and political critique that we continue to believe, is a unique, important, and maybe lifesaving role to play.

Today, we are much less sanguine about identifying any century as "the Christian century." The twentieth century, in addition to a time of unprecedented and unimaginable advances in communication, travel, and health care, turned out also to be one of the most tragic of centuries in ways so familiar I do not need to document beyond two words: Holocaust and Hiroshima. At the end of the twentieth century, no one with their senses about them was suggesting that it was a Christian century or that the kingdom of God had finally come.

And yet, insofar as Christianity has to do with a radical, unconditional, healing Divine love incarnate, alive, active and working in human history, every century, including the twentieth, as well as this one, the twenty-first, is in fact a Christian century. Christ is present. The kingdom does come.

The one hundred plus essays selected for this book from the nearly four hundred that appeared in the *Christian Century* during my seventeen-year tenure as editor and publisher offer glimpses into a faith and church at the dawn of a new century. And what a time it was.

The approach of a new millennium inspired all sorts of apocalyptic fears to surface and the events of September 11, 2001, seemed tragically, appallingly, to fulfill the worst of those fears. The jet airliners, hijacked and crashed into the twin towers of the World Trade Center and Pentagon, exposed our vulnerability and a new word—terrorism—entered our vocabulary. The attacks sent shock waves through every aspect of American culture, setting off a wave of ugly Islamaphobia but also a new awareness that American Christians knew next to nothing about Islam, the mosque down the block, and their Muslim neighbors. The invasion of Afghanistan and Iraq and the subsequent discovery of secret prisons and enhanced interrogation, a euphemism for torture, prompted an important conversation about American values. In the Middle East, an actual two-state solution and peace between Israel and the Palestinians seemed tantalizingly possible for a while and then began to fade. American Protestant denominations were roiled by a profound conflict between their historic friendship with and support of Israel and long-standing commitments to mission partners in the area and to justice, peace, and security for all people. The issue of divestment also brought Christian congregations into sometimes difficult conversation and conflict with Jewish neighbors.

Nearly fifty years after the civil rights movement that was so important to the denominations, the nation elected Barack Obama, its first African American president. Issues that emerged during his presidency: reproductive freedom, gender equality, gay marriage, income equity, and increasing access to guns followed by horrific mass killings, all of which gathered passionate advocates from the religious community, on all sides of each issue.

My ecclesiastical home since birth has been in the historic mainline denominations, and those churches are also home to the vast majority of *Christian Century* readers. But the historical mainline churches have continued to see a steady decline in real numbers, dollars, and public posture and influence. Something was and is dying, and something is being born.

And now that I have retired from the pulpit and the editor's desk, the Chicago Cubs, baseball's loveable losers, playing major league baseball for 108 years without a World Series Championship in an extraordinary era of futility, are playing very good baseball in every dimension of the game and are a joy to watch. I have had fun, over the years, holding up my team as eloquent examples of Christian virtue: humility, steadfastness, patience, and long-suffering and everlasting hope. If they are as good as they seem in April of 2016, I will have to rethink an entire theological, existential paradigm, and I am happy to turn that critical task over to my successor.

I do not know what the remainder of the twenty-first century holds for the church. Somewhere between what I see and what I hope for is an emerging church that is incarnational in terms of its love for and involvement deeply in the life of the world; ecumenical in terms of relationships between churches, denominations, and communions, united in faith and hope and gratitude; and interfaith, open to the world and religious truth and practice of the world's people.

I think I see hints of what is coming. I have five adult children, all married, and thirteen grandchildren, all of them attending and involved in churches. One family is deeply committed to the parochial school their three daughters attend and the parish church they attend when they are not in Sunday school at Fourth Presbyterian. They simply don't seem to care at all about the historic reasons Catholics and Protestants have created to criticize and demean one another when they weren't engaged in killing one another. I was invited to participate in Ella's First Communion, and I did. Ella also received a Bible at Fourth Presbyterian—and her mother told me she keeps it under her pillow and sleeps on it. If we don't get in the way, they will show us how to be—how we are—one holy catholic church.

Two of our families are becoming disillusioned and impatient with their church because, until recently, it was not very welcoming to a daughter and a sister because of sexual orientation. They simply can't fathom why the decision to include all people is so difficult for some faith communities. I pray every day that we won't lose them, that they won't give up on the church while it continues to wrestle with the issue. When my adult children heard that I would be going to yet another meeting to talk about gender and sexual orientation equality in the church, they said, in unison, "Dad! Are you still talking about that? Don't you know that the world has moved on?" Even Pope Francis gets it.

Whatever church emerges as the twenty-first century continues will have gotten past the public battle over the "hot button" issues and will, I hope and pray, be as shockingly open to the world and as radically inclusive as its Lord was. Whatever church manages to live into the future will be a lot less obsessive about guarding its traditions and getting its rules and doctrines right than it is about getting Jesus right when he sat down at the table, broke bread, and drank wine with the many people his religion regarded as unfit and unclean.

What the world sees of religion is mostly disgraceful. So, dear friends, do not let go of the vision—the hope—that we believe is in the heart of God—for the unity of the church. It was this vision of the oneness of the church that inspired Charles Clayton Morrison, the new owner and editor of the *Christian Century* at the 1910 Edinburgh Missionary Conference. Morrison's new project would be, from the beginning, an intentionally ecumenical journal. He called it "undenominational." For more than a century, the magazine simply assumed, in spite of the divisiveness and diversity spawned by the Protestant Reformation, that the church of Jesus Christ transcends human imagination and human structures and is one, holy, and catholic.

That ecumenical vision was never merely a fad. It is there from the evening Jesus told his disciples that their oneness with him and with one another was the way that the truth about him would be visible. There is and has always been an evangelical imperative about ecumenism at the *Christian Century*. While reporting and commenting on issues of importance to people of faith, it has maintained its founding commitment to the oneness of the church.

It has been my honor to be affiliated for the past seventeen years with this journal that I have read and relied on for the entirety of my ministry and to work with gifted, committed colleagues devoted to the magazine's liveliness and relevance and to its mission of helping readers in the adventure of "thinking critically and living faithfully." I am grateful particularly to David Heim, whose wise faithfulness has shaped the magazine's content, and to Jason Byassee, former assistant editor, pastor, and academic who graciously agreed to write the generously perceptive introduction to each section, and to Jessica Miller Kelley and the good folk at Westminster John Knox Press for skilled and faithful editing.

I dedicate this book to the people of the Fourth Presbyterian Church of Chicago, who allowed me the time to go to work for the *Christian Century* while serving as their pastor, and to my wife, Sue, with deep gratitude for her grace and love and personal faithfulness, which have sustained me over the years and continue, happily, today.

1
The Mainline and the World

MAINLINE CHURCHES in this country were built to rule. Sometimes called the "seven sisters" (Methodist, American Baptist, Presbyterian, Lutheran, Episcopalian, Disciples of Christ, and United Church of Christ), they are heirs to the magisterial Reformation churches in Europe where they were often official state churches (Lutherans in Scandinavia; Presbyterians in Scotland and Switzerland and the Netherlands; Anglicans in England). In mid-twentieth-century America they had each built enormous infrastructure with corporate offices and heads of this and that division. They looked like a branch of the U.S. government, or a Big Three Detroit automaker, or a big box department store.

John Buchanan rose to positions of prominence in this mainline tradition. He became pastor at Fourth Presbyterian Church, a congregation of over five thousand members and a prime example of the mainline "tall-steeple" downtown church, with its gothic revival architecture and inclusion on the National Register of Historic Places. He served as moderator of the Presbyterian Church (U.S.A.), a position long held by master pulpiteers and consensus builders and public spokespeople. He also became editor/publisher of the *Christian Century*, a magazine that was founded by Disciples of Christ and is trusted by members of all mainline denominations long after shedding its Disciples affiliation.

1

His career spans the time between the mainline denominations' ascendancy and its descent, exemplified here in his attendance at the Chicago Federation of Churches' annual meeting and banquet as a student in 1960, attended by Mayor Daley and other dignitaries, and his later vote to usher the same body out of existence in 1986, once he'd returned to the city to be the pastor of Fourth Presbyterian.

What do churches built to rule do with themselves when they no longer rule? When the country for which they intend to be the soul no longer knows they're there?

As these essays make clear, they don't go away quietly. They remember their purpose—which from the beginning was to nurture churches for faithful living in the world. They don't go hide in bunkers or silos. They rather make friends in unlikely places, build consensus where possible, point out public lunacies and fallacies, and show what light their worship of Jesus throws on the world's goings on. And if John's voice is any indication, they do so with a smile, without anxiety or hand-wringing, and with positive joy.

THE NEXT CHRISTIAN CENTURY

March 3, 1999[1]

This magazine has been a friend and a resource for me for 35 years. It has stimulated my thinking, encouraged me professionally and personally, challenged my assumptions, introduced me to new movies, books and authors, pricked my conscience, made me smile and, on occasion, made me angry. Come to think of it, my *Christian Century* subscription has been one of the best bargains around.

Like many readers, as soon as the *Century* arrived at my desk I checked to see what James Wall had to say about what's going on in the world and then turned immediately to the back to read Martin Marty's weekly gift of wry wit, wisdom and grace. Happily, they both will continue to write for our pages.

Since I am now personally invested in this enterprise, I have been wondering what the people who so confidently called their magazine the *Christian Century* in 1900 would think at the end of the 20th century. Many of them believed that the world would be Christian by the year 2000, and that the U.S. would be a nation shaped, formed and informed by what we now know as the liberal Protestant vision. We live, as this journal regularly reminds us, in a very different place than our forebears anticipated.

The issue for us is not how to organize and sustain a thoroughly Christian culture, but how to relate to a global and national culture that is thoroughly pluralistic. To put the question another way: How shall those of us who identify with the old mainline religious institutions relate to a culture that no longer always agrees with us and increasingly doesn't know what to make of us?

In his review in the February 3–10 issue of James Tunstead Burtchaell's *The Dying of the Light: The Disengagement of Colleges and Universities from Their Christian Churches*, Ralph Wood commented that the "effort to build up a great unified American civilization—indeed, to usher in the Christian century whence this journal takes its name—produced a huge unintended irony.[2] The old-line universities where Protestant liberalism was once the established faith became so all-inclusive that they not only lost their Christian identity, they eventually excluded Protestant liberalism." Burtchaell's description of what happened to Christian colleges and universities applies to much of the culture.

How to be Christian in a pluralistic society? How to be faithfully Christian in a world of competing truth claims, many of them vigorously winning adherents? One way, of course, is to hunker down, strengthen the walls, bar the gates, and prepare for a future of increasing cultural ambivalence and, eventually, hostility. Another approach, and the one that will characterize this journal, is to continue to engage the culture, issue by issue—and to be a place where Christians engage one another across the entire front of issues: theological, biblical, political, economic, social, aesthetic, ethical. And if we're not quite as confident about the outcome of our efforts as were our forebears, we're determined to be every bit as engaged in the world around us as they were.

There is some precedent, after all, for plunging ahead without knowing where the journey is headed, for setting off on a pilgrimage without a sure sense of what is around the next corner. At the heart of the faith we share is our trust that God is up to something in history—grand and small; global and personal—which we can't quite see or understand yet. And therefore there is a strong reason to keep calling this journal exactly what it has been called for 100 years, the *Christian Century*.

OVERCOMING DIVISION

January 3, 2001

Calendar purists insist that only now are we entering the 21st century, since 2000 was really the final year of the 20th century. Whichever it is, I entered this new year thinking a lot about the fractious divisiveness that seems so evident everywhere in the world, and about its reverse, the precious but fragile unity of the human family.

I recently had a unique experience which prompted some hopefulness about overcoming divisiveness. As a member of a committee of the Presbyterian Church (U.S.A.) which has been talking to representatives of the Vatican, I had the chance to meet with Cardinal Edward Cassidy, a delightful Australian who is the president of the Pontifical Council on Christian Unity, and with John Radano, an American staff member of the Pontifical Council. The discussion was part of a dialogue that developed in response to *Ut Unum Sint*, Pope John Paul II's 1995 encyclical that invited Christians to a renewed discussion of Christian unity. The Presbyterian-Vatican talks have focused in particular on the pope's stated intent to find "a new way of exercising primacy which, while in no way renouncing what is essential to its mission, is nonetheless open to a new situation." Cardinal Cassidy acknowledged that "the concept of the papacy is a difficulty—to some, insurmountable—for Protestants."

Some of the Presbyterians wondered, in the aftermath of Dominus Iesus—the Vatican statement that called non-Roman churches "not churches in the proper sense" and "defective"—whether our conversation was between "brothers and sisters in the Body of Christ." Cardinal Cassidy answered firmly and eagerly: "Yes—a very large Yes!"

Near the end of the deliberations, the stated clerk of the PCUSA, Clifton Kirkpatrick, observed that the 20th century was one of the most violent and divisive in all of human history. But God continues to call the church to a ministry of reconciliation. The 21st century, by God's grace, could be the century of reunion. I thought of the haunting words of Roman Catholic theologian Hans Kung:

> There will be no peace among the peoples of the world without peace among the world religions. There will be no peace among the world religions without peace among the Christian churches.[3]

I can't think of any project more important for the whole human race, all the religions of the world and all the Christian churches, including my own, as this new year begins, than making the 21st century the century of reconciliation and reunion.

NAME-CALLING

January 25, 2003

I began my ministry as a "new church development" pastor in a small town in northwest Indiana. The new congregation grew out of an older nondenominational church. When the time came to claim a name for our new adventure, we put together, in fine Presbyterian style, a small committee to study the matter and bring recommendations to the congregation.

I urged the committee to find a name for the congregation with biblical or historical meaning, and not simply follow the traditional Presbyterian custom of calling churches by the street on which they were located or, most common of all, First or Second Presbyterian. The committee listened patiently to their young pastor and assembled a list of names, including Immanuel, Trinity, Hope, Faith—my suggestions—and First Presbyterian—their unanimous choice. When the committee brought the report to the congregation, I made the case for Immanuel. ("God with us" what more fitting name for our church?) Someone observed that my suggestions sounded pretty Catholic or at least Lutheran. The vote was taken and First Presbyterian won hands down.

Historically Presbyterians have been the least imaginative of God's people about naming our churches. I grew up in Broad Avenue Presbyterian Church and have served a Broad Street, a Fourth and a First in addition to a Bethany.

With my memory and curiosity on this matter aroused by John Dart's article on church names ("What's in a Name: Mainliners ponder denominational labels"), I asked the national headquarters of the Presbyterian Church (U.S.A.) how many of its 11,178 congregations are named First Presbyterian Church. The answer staggered me. There are 2,610 of them—almost 25 percent of all PCUSA churches. That's a lot of unimagination. My guess is that it reflects our ancestors' antipathy toward Rome. Catholics call their churches Sacred Heart and Blessed Virgin. And Lutherans and Episcopalians adopt names like Trinity or name their churches after saints. Defiant Calvinists made their point by choosing First or Fifth Avenue.

As Dart observes, the inclination in some quarters now is to drop the denominational designation altogether. I fervently hope that doesn't happen, "Presbyterian" is difficult to spell and it's a lot easier to say simply "Fourth Church." But "Presbyterian" carries a lot of fascinating history, tradition and personality, and so does "Lutheran," "Methodist" and "Episcopal." Besides, I don't see people deciding to go to church or stay away on the basis of a name on the sign out front. That decision is made for other and more important reasons.

URBAN TURNAROUND: REORIENTING OLD CHURCHES FOR A NEW AGE OFTEN TAKES GREAT CREATIVITY

April 19, 2003

When Michael Harrington wrote *The Other America* 40 years ago, he pointed out that the advent of freeways linking suburban homes to downtown offices had rendered the poverty of the inner city invisible to many Americans. The city had become the home of the poor, the disadvantaged and the disenfranchised.

Since then there have been some important efforts to reclaim the possibilities and the promise of cities—part of a movement sometimes called the New Urbanism. Two articles in this issue make it clear that beneath the planning, zoning and development issues identified by the New Urbanism lie moral, spiritual and theological issues about what a community is and can be. So far, not many religious voices have taken part in the conversation.

That's odd because we were there from the beginning. One of the first buildings constructed in towns and cities was a church—a place for worship and where basic human community is formed. And we're still there, in the center of big cities and scattered throughout urban neighborhoods. On a ride on the Kennedy Expressway from O'Hare Airport to downtown Chicago you can see a series of wonderful old churches, massive basilicas built a century ago for the immigrant neighborhoods of Chicago.

Many of those old churches are very difficult to staff and maintain. One of the real challenges is that they were built for another era. The automobile and suburban sprawl changed everything for city churches.

A congregation I served in Columbus, Ohio, had to be virtually turned around because of the automobile. Members used to walk to church or were dropped off at the ornate street-front entrance. But by the time I came to the church, nobody had used that entrance for 50 years. People drove to church, parked in the lot behind it, and entered through what had been designed as a service entrance. It required some architectural creativity to reorient the church for a new age.

Every urban church has challenges like that. The congregation I currently serve enjoys a Gothic building designed by Ralph Adams Cram, one of the premier architects of the first part of the 20th century. After 18 years it still takes my breath away when I walk in off Michigan

Avenue, through the small entryway, into the narthex and then enter the soaring heights of our worship space. But it never occurred to Cram that a bride might want to get into that narthex without walking outside through a Chicago gale, or that people who come to worship might need to use a rest room. These are some of the challenges that are part of being a church in the city—challenges well worth meeting for the great privilege of being a church in such a place.

EVANGELICAL IMPERATIVE: KINDNESS, FORBEARANCE, GRACE

August 10, 2004

A recent editorial in *Christianity Today* suggested that "it may be time for mainline churches to consider an amicable divorce."[4] The editorial cited a proposal floated informally at the United Methodist General Conference in May to "explore an amicable and just separation" that would free the church from its "cycle of pain and conflict." Similar talk is heard regularly in Presbyterian circles, usually, but not exclusively, on the right. The pain and conflict is over issues of sexuality, particularly the issue of gay/lesbian ordination.

The editorial went on to suggest that the theology of mainline churches is shaped by a quest for self-realization and freedom of choice, and it declared that "large sections of the mainline churches" exhibit a "sub-Christian religion."

There is plenty to critique in these churches—but there is plenty of "sub-Christian religion" in the evangelical world as well. It's usually easier to see the fault in the other side than in one's own. That's precisely why it's important to stay with one another in spite of our failures and differences, trusting in the reconciling promise of the gospel. That's why some of us place a premium on the unity of the church.

There hasn't been a day in the past ten years that I haven't wished I belonged to a church that wasn't fighting and arguing. But I stay with it, and many thousands like me stay with their ecclesiastical families, because we believe our Lord wants us to, and that he was serious when he prayed for the oneness of his disciples "so that the world may believe."

The unity of the church is an evangelical imperative. If we can't hang together through the disagreements we face, why would the world take our gospel of reconciliation seriously?

I was at this year's Presbyterian General Assembly—the occasion on which we do our fighting annually. Actually, this was the last annual meeting: the assembly will meet biennially from now on, at least in part because it cuts in half the time and resources people invest in the fight. This assembly did what Presbyterian assemblies have done a lot recently: elected a moderator who is progressive on the ordination issue and then voted to retain the constitutional prohibition against ordaining sexually active gays and lesbians.

When Presbyterian ministers are ordained they promise to "further the peace, unity and purity of the church." It's difficult to have all three, but surely the church's unity is no less important that its peace and purity. I think the world is tired of our bickering and name-calling. I think the most compelling evangelical gesture we could make would be the demonstration of kindness, forbearance and grace inside and between the churches.

APPLAUDING DIVERSITY: ENOUGH OF ONE-RELIGION NATIONALISM

August 24, 2004

Protestants are about to become a minority in the U.S. after almost four centuries of numerical superiority and cultural dominance. A new study by the National Opinion Research Center reports that by the end of the year Protestants will probably make up less than 50 percent of the population.

The proportion of Roman Catholics in the population has remained stable at 25 percent. And the overwhelming majority of Americans continue to identify themselves as Christian.

So what is happening? The data suggest that the population cohort that is significantly growing is those who declare no religious affiliation.

That suggests that people are dropping out of churches, or that young adults are taking their traditional leave of absence from organized religion and not returning as they used to.

Another interesting thing has been happening as well, namely a dramatic increase in the nation's religious diversity. And that, I maintain, is a good thing. In fact, I'm proud of that. The world has had quite enough of one-religion nationalism recently.

Two hundred twenty-eight years ago the Founders who gathered in Philadelphia could have created a "Protestant nation" or a "Christian nation," but they didn't. Thirteen years later they formulated a constitution that included the radical concept of a religiously neutral state, a state in which citizens would be free to choose their religious commitments or choose not to be religious at all. Many people at the time thought that Thomas Jefferson's "fair experiment" would not work. But it did, in spite of persistent efforts over the centuries to turn us into a "Christian nation" or a "Judeo-Christian nation," despite battles over issues like whether the Ten Commandments should be posted in a courtroom.

That precious religious liberty is one of the best things about this country. If surrendering majority status is one of the results, I applaud it.

AN EVANGELICAL IMPERATIVE: CHRISTIAN UNITY

August 9, 2005

George Lindbeck's thoughtful reflections in this issue on the state of ecumenism set me to ruminating on my own ecumenical experience. It also reminded me that this journal has been ecumenically minded from its inception. For a time it even described itself as an "ecumenical weekly" (and before that as an "undenominational weekly").

My initial exposure to ecumenism occurred in the fall of my first year in seminary when my wife and I were asked to represent the University of Chicago Divinity School at the Church Federation of Chicago's annual meeting. We dressed up in our best clothes, took the train into the Loop, and found our way to the big hotel ballroom, the poshest space we had ever been in. We joined a huge throng of people festively gathered around tables with white tablecloths, centerpieces and more silverware than seemed necessary.

Seated at the head table were some of the most influential city leaders, including Mayor Richard J. Daley, who spoke about how important the Church Federation was to the city. It was a racially diverse gathering, and a speaker from the National Council of Churches talked about the civil rights movement and the critical role the ecumenical churches were playing in it. I was inspired. I thought I had experienced a little bit of God's kingdom on earth.

Ecumenism has been part of my ministry in each congregation I have served. I found the post-Vatican II openness between Protestants and Catholics bracing and exciting. When a Roman Catholic campus pastor at Purdue and I engaged in a dialogue sermon at an ecumenical service, it made the front page of the local newspaper.

When I returned to Chicago 25 years after seminary, I happily accepted a position on the board of that same Church Federation. At one of the first meetings I attended, we voted on a resolution to declare bankruptcy and dissolve the organization. Two mission units— a broadcast ministry and an anti-hunger program—were spun off, and they continue to do good work. But the disappearance of the Church Federation means there is no citywide organization or event that brings congregations together.

I miss the old structures, though I understand why they ran out of steam. Interfaith issues loomed and, as Lindbeck observes, the old ecumenical movement never did include evangelicals, Pentecostals and Roman Catholics. What I lament most, next to the fact that there is no large, public symbolic gathering of churches, is that the unity we seek seems more and more fragile within our own denominational families.

Christian unity is a gift we are given and which we can graciously receive and practice, or refuse. Unity is at least as important as the peace and purity of the church—something we Presbyterians promise at our ordinations to promote. Paul, in 1 Corinthians, and Jesus, in his prayer that his disciples might be one "so that the world may believe," understood the evangelical imperative of Christian unity. Part of our witness is that in Jesus Christ we belong together whether we want to or not.

LIVING TRADITIONS

February 23, 2011

I read the *Wall Street Journal* not daily but frequently, and while I appreciate the breadth of the coverage and the quality of the writing, I often find something to fuss with on the editorial pages. In the case of Russell D. Moore's article "Where have all the Presbyterians gone? Nondenominational churches are the fastest growing in the country," it seemed again as if the paper's editors, particularly the one who created the headline, are gleeful about the travails of mainline Protestant churches.[5] And it appears that someone has decided that Presbyterianism can stand for what is wrong in mainline churches, especially with their propensity to adopt progressive political views—in opposition to the *Journal*'s.

Despite the headline, Moore, dean of the Southern Baptist Theological Seminary in Louisville, Kentucky, never mentions Presbyterians except in a list of denominations with which fewer and fewer American Christians identify. "Are we witnessing the death of America's denominations?" Moore asks, and he points out that "more and more Christians choose a church not on the basis of its denomination" but on the basis of practical matters such as the nursery and the music. This is not new information. Every sociologist of religion I know relates that shift to our individualistic, consumer culture.

In *The Jesus Way*, Eugene Peterson says that "the great American innovation in congregation is to turn it into a consumer enterprise. It didn't take long for some of our brothers and sisters to develop consumer congregations . . . [that convey] the gospel in consumer terms: entertainment, satisfaction, excitement, adventure, problem solving, whatever." But as Peterson concludes, "This is not the way God brings us into conformity with the life of Jesus."

Moore claims that the huge success of the nondenominational megachurch is "a natural extension of the American evangelical experiment." I don't think so. I think it's about smart marketing and multiple options. Moore says post-World War II evangelicals and revivalists saw churches shift from sending missionaries to producing position papers on energy policy. That's a cheap shot. And even his denomination is starting to pay attention to the care of God's creation.

Moore points out that along with the growth of nondenominational churches, Southern Baptists have become the nation's largest

Protestant denomination. Then he comes to the bottom line: "Many of us believe denominations can represent fidelity to living traditions of local congregations that care about what Jesus cared about—personal conversion, discipleship, mission and community." Moore is confident that such is the case with the Southern Baptist Convention.

Many of us love the denominations that nurtured us, introduced us to Jesus and taught us how to follow him. We're part of families of faith with distinct customs, vocabularies and traditions of music. We try to express our discipleship in ecclesiastical structures that may not be as slick or as nimble as some independent enterprises—but we're trying to be faithful partners with thousands of other congregations that are trying to be faithful in the settings in which they find themselves, however difficult.

I'm weary of being lectured about what's wrong with mainline churches, but grateful for signs of honest inquiry and discernment from those in my church and others. And I'm grateful for Moore's hopeful conclusion: "Perhaps the denominational era has just begun."

SHARED MEAL

September 26, 2013

World Communion Sunday is one of the best ideas Presbyterians ever had. The idea originated in the 1930s, a time of economic turmoil and fear and the rise of militaristic fascism abroad. Hugh Thomson Kerr, a beloved pastor in the Presbyterian Church, persuaded the denomination to designate one Sunday when American Christians would join brothers and sisters around the world at the Lord's Table.

The idea caught on. Other denominations followed suit and the Federal Council of Churches (now the National Council of Churches) endorsed World Communion Sunday in 1940. But though the day is still noted in some denominational calendars and program materials, it doesn't seem to be considered as important as it once was.

Of course, every Sunday is in a sense World Communion Sunday insofar as many churches celebrate the Lord's Supper every Sunday. But we do not welcome one another at the Lord's Table. In some churches, a place at the table is reserved for members only.

Some Lutherans exclude other Lutherans. And, of course, Eucharist is restricted in the Roman Catholic tradition (although individual Catholic clergy do not always adhere to their church's teaching on this point).

I have heard all the ecclesiastical reasons for excluding people from the sacrament. I was once part of a Presbyterian delegation to a Reformed–Roman Catholic dialogue at the Vatican. Our delegation decided to gently raise the issue of sacramental exclusion. We agreed with our Catholic counterparts that the church has been given responsibility for the sacrament. As we pressed this issue, it became clear that we had not resolved disagreements about the nature of the church. Lewis Mudge, a Presbyterian theologian, spoke up: "You're still saying that we are not a true church, aren't you?" We remained, for them, an "ecclesial community," not a church—so no sharing of communion.

I believe that when Jesus said, "Do this in remembrance of me," he referred not only to the Last Supper but to his entire life of teaching, healing and welcoming all—a welcome so radical it scandalized religious leaders. I have never been able to square excluding a fellow Christian from the table and the meal that commemorates Jesus and that conveys, in bread and wine, something of his grace and love and forgiveness.

During a summer stint at a tiny church in Scotland, I had a visit from the pastor of the church in the next village who told me a communion story I will never forget.

He was an infantryman in the British army in World War II and ended up in a prisoner-of-war camp in Poland. The conditions were dreadful. There was no heat, and prisoners were given a single bowl of thin soup and a small crust of bread daily. Men were starving, sick, filthy and desperate. Suicide was a very real option. All one had to do was run toward the perimeter of the camp and leap against the barbed wire fence. Guards would immediately shoot and kill anyone trying to escape.

In the middle of the night he walked to the perimeter and sat down beside the fence to think about going through with it. He heard movement in the darkness from the other side of the fence. It was a Polish farmer. The man thrust his hand through the barbed wire and handed my friend half of a potato. In heavily accented English he said, "The Body of Christ."

"Do this in remembrance of me."

EMBARGOED PENSIONS

February 18, 2015

I visited Cuba 19 years ago, long before the recent softening of relationships between the Cuban and American governments. As a representative of the Presbyterian Church (U.S.A.), I was visiting the Independent Presbyterian Reformed Church of Cuba, which was established by Protestant missionaries in the late 19th century. The IPR churches had thrived over the years and had built a theological seminary at Matanzas.

After Cuba became a communist state the churches learned how to exist under the Castro regime's strictures and subtle—and sometimes not so subtle—persecution. There were some arrests and imprisonments. Churches were mostly allowed to remain open, but evangelism efforts were forbidden, and it was almost impossible to print and distribute literature. Government agents often came to worship services; a Christian's public affirmation of faith could have economical, professional, and educational consequences.

At the time of our visit a warming of the relationship between the two nations had come to a sudden end, and there was a reemergence of suspicion, hostility, and fear. Despite these demanding and sometimes dangerous circumstances, Cuban Christians had remained faithful to their Christian commitments and their churches.

Then I made a distressing discovery. The Cuban Presbyterian Church was formerly an organic part of PCUSA, and Cuban pastors had paid into the Presbyterian Pension and Benefits Plan—but they weren't receiving the benefits. After the Castro revolution, the assets of American corporations that were doing business in Cuba were expropriated, and our government placed an economic embargo on Cuba. Suddenly 50 retired Cuban pastors and church workers were deprived of their pension benefits.

For many years the Presbyterian Board of Pensions worked to persuade our government to allow the board to make payments. The legal issue was acquiring licenses that are required to make monetary payments to Cuban nationals or to release money from accounts held in the United States in their names.

Meanwhile the money sat in U.S. accounts where it increased in value to nearly a million dollars. But that money was not getting into the hands of the people who had earned it.

Presbyterian Pension Board officials would not give up. Frank Maloney, chief operating officer of the Board of Pensions, went to work with legal counsel Jean Hemphill. They continued to request the release of the funds and were denied each time by the Office of Foreign Assets Control of the U.S. Treasury Department. PCUSA Board officials and officers visited U.S. lawmakers—only to encounter the strong anti-Castro lobby in Congress that opposes any political or economic accommodation with the Castro government or the Cuban people.

Progress came in the mid-1990s when a license was issued to pay the Cuban retirees $100 per month, but it was still held up by the prohibition against U.S. banks doing business in Cuba. In the meantime, retired Cuban pastors were aging and starting to die. In 2006 the government licensed the church to pay up to $500 per month and permitted board staff to travel to Cuba to find the pensioners and their survivors.

Now, in the new atmosphere in U.S.-Cuban relations initiated by the Obama administration, the blocked accounts will be opened and full payment made to surviving Cuban pastors and their heirs.

The mainline denominational agency's faithfulness and relentless commitment to justice reinforces my conviction that these structures do absolutely critical work and faithful mission.

Meanwhile, the Cuban church has pointed the way to faithful work with its courageous and durable witness. During visits nearly two decades ago and again in 2001, I developed ongoing friendships with Cuban pastors and church leaders. My experiences in worship, preaching, and baptizing a Cuban infant were inspiring.

The Christians in Cuba have carried on. They are still there. There is, I think, something in Jesus' promise to Peter that the gates of hell will not prevail against the church.

2
Ministry and Church Life

BECAUSE MAINLINE CHURCHES were designed to rule, or at least to advise those who did, we have had the luxury of speaking as though Congress is on speed dial, waiting to hear what we think. This is why John Buchanan's essays on ministry and church life are so important. The Century's primary readers have long been pastors who do the day-in, day-out, workaday, unglamorous job of serving God's people. While John's life may have been somewhat different than most, with a five-thousand-member congregation on Chicago's Gold Coast, its fundamental form was not. He preached and prayed and supervised and presided and fretted over the budget and washed feet.

There is a deep dignity to the essays in this section. They show that Buchanan honored the form of life he shared with his readers. Church bureaucrats and professors (of which I am one!) are often members of the church alumni club—carping safely from the sidelines, as though if we deigned to do the job we'd have all the answers. But no one does—not to the questions that matter. Parish ministry is really hard. One aspect of the shift from Christendom to post-Christendom is a drying up of benefits that once lubricated that life, made its functioning a little easier on the joints (free tickets, rounds of golf, meals, respectful interactions with strangers and casual acquaintances). In the recent film *Calvary*, Catholic priest Father James (Brendan Gleeson) is walking with a little girl in his village, having an avuncular chat, when her father pulls up in a car, terrified. He yanks her away as though the priest were a convicted pedophile—which, given all he ever hears about the church through his media, the priest must be. That's the shift from Christendom to post—from a world where benefits unsought fall in clergy's laps to one where we're guilty of something unspeakable just by turning up in a collar.

John points out with Mike Royko that air-conditioning may have killed social capital in the United States. Neighbors used to sweat outdoors together on porches. Now they're shut tightly inside climate-controlled rooms talking to no one, absorbed in TV. The pastor's job is more important and difficult than ever—to extol the value of community to people who'd prefer their own comfortable loneliness. That's unimaginably difficult. But to see it as John Buchanan does, it's also a deep joy.

These essays tell a bittersweet truth about the life of a pastor. For all its drudgery and problems, it is shot through with radiance, suspended in glory. And, to hear John tell it, it's a vocation resplendent with light. One senses, with Yogi Berra (see John? I can quote baseball dignitaries too!) that if John had it to do all over again, he'd do it all over again.

CLEAR CALLINGS

November 1, 2000

For many of us, the call to ministry comes in stages.

The reflection on vocation in this issue by Gilbert Meilaender ("Divine Summons") takes us from Vergil's epic, the *Aeneid*, to the Reformation era to the 20th century, with many stops in between. He prodded me, as I'm sure he will others, to think more deeply about their own sense of vocation.

Happy is the one to whom God speaks in a clear, unmistakable voice with specific instructions about what to do with his or her life. Some folk I know experienced a call to their vocation like that. Most did not. My experience of a call to ministry came in stages, at different times and places, none of them startlingly clear—a door opening unexpectedly here, another door closing disappointingly there. At first it was an intellectual itch I couldn't scratch. A college adviser urged me to take a year to examine my intellectual and spiritual questions seriously. At the end of the year, I knew that I wanted to pursue the questions as far as I could.

I have on occasion felt in the depths of my soul the rightness of that long-ago decision to be a minister and lifelong asker of the big questions: at the baptism of a child, during a memorial service when the congregation gathers to celebrate the good life of one of its own, at the end of an exhausting Sunday when I have been privileged to witness the church acting like the body of Christ, during the opening hymn in worship when we stand and sing with the glorious organ carrying us, "Praise Ye the Lord, who o'er all things so wondrously reigneth . . . Hast thou not seen, How thy desires e'er have been, Granted in what He Ordaineth?" But it doesn't happen a lot, and certainly not with the clarity of a voice calling my name in the night.

Meanwhile, I think of my father, who worked all his life at a job he did not like. It provided a living for our family, but very little by way of emotional satisfaction. It would not have occurred to him to define his labor as God's call. His vocation, I have concluded, was to be a lover of life, a prod and challenge and inspiration to his sons.

I'm grateful for the blessing of being paid to do what I believe I am called to do. I'm particularly grateful for all those who seek and find their vocation when it is not what they must do for a living.

This is also the place to say I'm grateful for those whose vocation of serving the church and the world includes being an editor at large for this magazine. With this issue we welcome an expanded list of these thinkers and writers, whose willingness to share their insights and energies are crucial to the life of this magazine.

MEGACHURCH, MINI-CONGREGATION

April 10, 2002

This issue features a topic in which I have a personal interest—the megachurch (see John Dart's article, "Wanted: Megapastors"), though I deplore the term and try never to use it. It is such a market-oriented word, so hurtful to the vast majority of ministers who work faithfully in congregations that do not approach "mega" dimensions except in spirit, courage, compassion and mission.

My special interest in John Dart's report comes also from my friendship with the late Frank Harrington, who before he died unexpectedly and much too soon was the pastor of the largest congregation in my denomination. Atlanta's Peachtree Presbyterian Church at one time listed 13,000 members. Dart quotes Jerry Van Marter, the Presbyterian communications officer, to the effect that Harrington resisted deleting a single name from the church roll. I would add that Frank Harrington was a terrific pastor, that he loved the Presbyterian Church, and that he led his congregation to impressive commitment to mission in new church development and in Habitat for Humanity projects, and was a major contributor to theological education.

Our article on megachurch leadership revived a mental conversation I had been having with Eugene Peterson, who was interviewed in our previous issue about pastoral ministry. Peterson declared that "pastoral work is best handled in a fairly small setting," and he specified that "fairly small" means "somewhere between 50 and 500 people." I bristled a bit at this, but eventually concluded that he is right. Good pastoral work happens in settings of under 500 people. If your congregation is larger than that, then it's important to do something to create the dynamic of a smaller congregation.

I view my congregation as a network of smaller congregations, organized around fellowship, mission, education or personal need. And I regard my pastoral colleagues as pastors of those individual congregations. My task is to oversee the network of congregations and pay special attention to my colleagues—the staff itself being one of those smaller congregations of the church.

Peterson is right about the numbers. One person can be pastor to up to 500 people. Beyond 500, the inevitable bureaucratization will begin to work against community and pastoral care. When I was a pastor of a congregation of 100 people, I quickly knew every family and every member well and visited every home. In a church of 500, it took eight years before I knew every member and had visited their homes. In a church of 1,200, I eventually knew most of the people, and visited in a few homes. Now, serving a congregation approaching 5,000 members, I am gratified that the vast majority of those members are known by one of the church's ministers.

But every Sunday after worship I see the smaller congregations gather in the corners of the sanctuary and throughout the building. Animated conversations begin to happen and lives are touched by the grace of God communicated in and through a small group, one of the many congregations in which pastoral care can and does happen.

START-UP FAITH: A CONFIRMATION CONUNDRUM

October 4, 2003

At one of our church's weekly staff meetings the youth minister said he had a problem and needed his colleagues' advice. In the course of teaching the confirmation class, he had asked the young people to write their own statement of faith. The problem, he said, was that one of the students didn't believe much of anything, though he was happily involved in the confirmation process. The question our colleague posed for us was elegantly simple: "Can you be confirmed in this church if you don't believe in God?"

What ensued was a wide-ranging and good conversation. Positions ranged from "Of course not! Belief in God is basic to all the rest. You can't possibly be a confirmed church member if you don't believe" to "Of course! Why not? Jesus never asked his disciples to write a credo. He simply invited them to follow, and they did. Who knows what they believed about God?"—with all points in between. The question pushed us to think not only about the purpose of confirmation, but about the aims of youth ministry. What exactly do we hope to accomplish?

The discussion prompted me to reminisce about the youth programs I encountered growing up. My experience was probably typical of most Presbyterians of that time. There simply wasn't much for us. We went to church with our parents, attended Sunday school, and were confirmed while in junior high—in my case, by memorizing the Westminster Shorter Catechism and then reciting questions and answers for the Session during Holy Week. It wasn't until I attended church camp one summer that I discovered a community beyond the walls of my home congregation. (At camp I also discovered that being a young Christian did not preclude having a little fun—there were softball games, a swimming pool and girls.)

My youth experience was considerably enriched by regular attendance, with my next-door-neighbor chums, at Baptist Young People's Union on Sunday evenings, because there wasn't much happening at my own church. The Baptists had lively music—"I've got the joy, joy, joy, joy, down in my heart!"—as well as Bible memorization competitions, food and hay rides.

Looking back, I'm glad my confirmation experience did not require me to write a personal credo. I'm sure I would have come up with something acceptable, but I doubt very much that it would have had much authenticity. I was interested in Jesus and I liked church—and that was pretty much it. My faith was at an early stage of a long, evolutionary process which continues still, and I look back with gratitude at all the experiences along the way.

I am greatly heartened that some of the church's best and brightest people are putting their intelligence and imagination to the ongoing task of being the church for and with young people. They are seeking to help youth formulate their faith—but not necessarily in verbal formulas. Several articles in this issue remind us of how challenging this work is—and how exciting and important.

By the way, we did confirm the agnostic.

HANGING OUT: CONGREGATIONS ARE LIFE-SAVING COMMUNITIES

February 10, 2004

References to Robert Putnam have turned up in many sermons in recent years, including my own, because of a timely observation he made, one that immediately resonated with pastors as both true and important. America, he said, was experiencing a sharp decline in "social capital," by which he meant the tangible and intangible benefits of community involvement. (See our interview with Putnam, "Let's Meet: Rebuilding Community.")

Pastors understood exactly what Putnam was saying. We know that modern life seems almost to constitute a conspiracy against community. We know how many people live isolated lives, apart from family, friends and neighbors. When people are watching four hours of television per day, on top of an eight- or ten-hour work day, there is not much time left for relating to others or building community. And I know plenty of people who spend their nonworking hours online, which, though potentially a way to stay in touch with people, remains a solitary activity.

The late *Chicago Tribune* columnist Mike Royko used to quip that what destroyed community was air-conditioning. Before AC, Royko said, people would sit on their front porches or front stoops to enjoy the relative cool of the evening, and they inevitably talked to one another.

Royko's theory evoked my own sweet memories of summer evenings, sitting in our backyard listening to my father and the next-door neighbor discuss an amazing variety of topics on which they both had opinions—from the progress of our tomato plants to the imminent threat of a Soviet nuclear attack to the wretched state of both political parties. (When I wasn't doing that, I was sitting on the front porch with the Philco radio tuned to the Pittsburgh Pirates' game—the broadcast eerily echoing from every other porch on the block.)

Putnam says that "the biggest task of pastors is to build connections"—build social capital. That's a relatively new development. My father, who was so garrulous with our neighbors in their summer evening colloquies, never looked to the church for community. Today, with the air-conditioning on, the house tightly shut and the TV on, the church would be almost all he would have in the way of a community.

Church connections are all that many people have. Congregations are often life-saving communities for people like that, especially in times of crisis. Putnam reminds us that creating and nurturing community is not only a relevant task, but one that is basic to our health and identity.

EDIFICE COMPLEX? SUBLIME ARCHITECTURE

June 15, 2004

Scripture assures us that "we have a building from God, a house not made with hands, eternal in the heavens" (2 Cor. 5:1). But pastors and lay leaders end up spending a lot of time fussing with the church structures—the "physical plant," as we have learned to call it. Designing, building and maintaining structures have occupied the church's attention, inspired its imagination, and called forth labor and sacrifice perhaps more than any other set of tasks.

Most of us feel a little guilty about that overwhelming commitment to buildings, our "edifice complex." We tell people over and over that the building is not the church; the people are the church, the *ekklesia*, the called-out, beloved community. We say that we could do just fine without the building, in fact might even be freed up to be a more faithful church if we didn't have to maintain the building. People listen to us respectfully but remain unconvinced.

Some of the worst moments and most painful conflicts occur because of buildings. Do we redecorate, and how? Expand, renovate or reconfigure? Replace carpet? Tear down and start again? Shutter, sell and close? Pity the pastor who does not appreciate the importance of the building, and the significance the church's people attach to it.

Roman Catholics and Episcopalians don't seem to have the same hang-ups about buildings that we descendants of the Puritans do. We have something of a love-hate relationship with our real estate, and we're pretty sure that of all the idolatries the church is prone to, the idolizing of one's building is the worst. A Calvinist visiting St. Peter's in Rome experiences a spiritual crisis, a wrenching conflict between an appreciation of all the beauty and a suspicion that someone made a very big mistake here.

Church buildings, regardless of their age, style and size, say something about what happens in them and also around them. I heard Jean Bethke Elshtain say one time that the mere existence of a church building, even a closed one, has a measurably healthy affect on its community. Roger Kennedy, in his handsome book *American Churches*, writes that church buildings are a reminder of an "alternate way of stating reality." I'm reminded of that observation every day when I report for work in an English Gothic cathedral-type building nestled between skyscrapers, four-star hotels and expensive department stores.

Pastors, church leaders, and anyone who thinks and cares about churches, cities and neighborhoods will profit from Gretchen Buggeln's reflections on four recent books on church architecture ("Sacred Spaces"). I will suggest one more book: Ross King's *Brunelleschi's Dome*, the fascinating story of one of the world's artistic and engineering miracles, the dome of Santa Maria del Fiore in Florence, completed in 1436. The architecture is so sublime that Michelangelo arranged to be buried just inside the front door of Florence's Santa Croce so that on resurrection day the first sight he saw would be Felippo Brunelleschi's dome.

ALL TOGETHER NOW: THE POWER AND BEAUTY OF SHARING MUSIC

July 25, 2006

"O sing to the Lord a new song," the psalmist urges. I've always imagined someone in the back pew saying, "There's nothing wrong with the old song."

The conversation with songwriter John Bell ("Sing a New Song") in this issue takes us inevitably into the "worship wars," in which music is one of the battlefields. Bell is an accomplished musician whose compositions, like the music of the Iona community, of which he is a member, is inventive, theologically authentic and musically strong.

Church music says something about our ecclesiology and our Christology, not to mention our anthropology and aesthetics. When we argue over whether to sing Bach or praise choruses, we are also arguing about the nature of the church and the authenticity of its witness.

Music is powerful. Parents sing to infants from birth. Mothers-to-be play music for their babies in utero. One of my most poignant memories is of my infant granddaughter lying in the hospital after open-heart surgery with tubes and wires connecting her to a battery of monitors. The doctors had literally paralyzed her to allow her heart to heal. The mobile fastened to her crib softly played, over and over, a Mozart divertimento.

For ministers, music is often the essence of worship. We're so focused on the mechanics of the liturgy and on the sermon that it's the music that carries us along. Dostoevsky said somewhere that when his faith faltered and he found himself doubting, the music of the church and the singing of the congregation held him up. William Sloane Coffin wrote about music: "In times of desolation, God alone has comforted me more; and when the world seems bent on madness, it's music as much as literature that reassures me of its sanity."

Bell observes that church is about the only place in our culture where people still sing together. There is at least one more place: Wrigley Field, where in the middle of the seventh inning people sing "Take Me Out to the Ballgame." That tradition was started by the late sportscaster Harry Caray, and now the singing is led by different celebrities, some of whom can sing and some of whom cannot. Nevertheless, everybody sings and it makes for a wonderful experience.

Many of the battles over music are battles over different musical idioms. I have found that jazz is an idiom that lends itself to liturgy, and that many jazz musicians understand what liturgy is about and can make meaningful, joyful, evocative music.

I recently preached at the pastoral installation of a friend. I saw in the bulletin that the response to the benediction was going to be "Take the A Train," a Duke Ellington classic. After he pronounced the benediction, the pastor invited everyone to be seated and then explained that when he moved to New York City to attend seminary, his mother warned him not to get on the wrong train. But he had learned that the nature of ministry is traveling to new places, meeting new people and being open to God's surprises. With that, a trumpet player and a pianist launched into one of the most spirited versions of "Take the A Train" I've ever heard. The mostly older congregation loved it. Heads began to nod, feet tapped, smiles broke out. It was a new song, at least in that context, and it was great.

SOMETHING CHRISTLIKE: A LIFE-GIVING STRATEGY

July 29, 2008

The version of Christianity that appears in the media often embarrasses me: it's narrow, sectarian, exclusive and sometimes mean-spirited. So it was a joy to find in the May 26 *New Yorker* an article by novelist Ian Frazier about a church being a church in the best sense.[1]

Frazier conducts a weekly writing workshop at a church soup kitchen in New York City, and he regularly encounters gifted men and women who, for one reason or another, are homeless and hungry. The Church of the Holy Apostles is a landmark, with a high arched ceiling and gorgeous stained-glass windows. Over the years the Episcopal congregation dwindled in size as the neighborhood changed until the 200 members could no longer afford to pay the bills to keep it going. A new rector suggested that "if Holy Apostles is going out of business, it might as well do some good before it does."

So in 1982 the church launched a free-lunch program. Thirty-five people showed up. The program grew and attracted more people and outside support. In a few years the congregation was serving 900 lunches daily and bursting the seams of its mission house.

In 1990, during roof repairs to the main sanctuary, a fire broke out that caused major damage. During insurance-covered restoration and renovation, and while the pews were out, members came up with an idea: Why not leave the pews out and use the worship space, which was empty and unused Monday through Friday, for the lunch program?

Now the church is serving 1,200 meals a day. Volunteers do most of the work. They take the tables down on Friday afternoon and set up folding chairs for the weekend. The budget is now $2.7 million, which comes from businesses, foundations, the city—and the 200 members, who, instead of closing down a church, are part of a vital and compelling community of faith.

The program rules are simple: no proselytizing and no one turned away. If anyone wants more food, that person can go outside, stand in line, get another ticket and eat again. Frazier asked Elizabeth Maxwell of the Holy Apostles staff about the religious motivation behind the program. She said: "Well, we do this because Jesus said to feed the hungry. There's no more to it than that. Jesus told us to take care of the poor and hungry and those in prison. . . . In all the intricacies of scriptural interpretation, that message—feed the hungry—could not be more clear. Those of us at Holy Apostles feel we have a Sunday-Monday connection. The bread and wine of the Eucharist we share on Sunday becomes the food we share with our neighbors during the week."

There has long been an important debate in the church about whether its mandate is to feed the hungry or to address the social, economic and political structures that cause people to be hungry. We are in a major global food crisis, the reasons for which are complex—including the rising cost of oil, which has an impact on the cost of fertilizer and transportation. It is a crisis that ultimately will not be addressed by food aid. If you want to take Jesus' moral imperative seriously, sooner or later you have to think about politics and economics.

In the meantime, it is important that the world see in the church something of the kindness, compassion and justice of Jesus which is behind the advocacy for social and political change. It's a matter of both/and.

Maybe the world would find churches more interesting and compelling if they showed something of the love of Jesus in their lives and practices. Maybe there is no more important and life-giving strategy for every church than finding something Christlike to do.

GRAVESIDE: THE BEST AND WORST OF MINISTRY

October 6, 2009

The articles in this issue on funerals set me to thinking about my own experience and the changes I have witnessed in funerals. In my first two congregations I never conducted a funeral in the church itself. Every funeral was held in a funeral home, and every funeral was followed by a graveside interment and committal. That meant taking a ride in the front seat of the hearse, making small talk with the funeral director, and being part of a long procession of cars led by a county sheriff on a motorcycle. Now the funerals I conduct are in the church, where they belong. Only rarely is there a casket present or a graveside committal. In downtown Chicago the last funeral home closed several years ago.

I'm not the first minister to observe that presiding at funerals represents both the best and worst of ministry. There is no greater honor than to be with a family during the sickness and death of one of its members, to pray at the bedside, to talk with people about life and death and to help a family plan a funeral service. The church is never more authentically the church than when it gathers to give thanks for the life of one of its own and commend his or her life to God's eternal love in the promise of the resurrection.

Ministers encounter many other approaches to funerals. In my study not long ago, adult sons and daughters began planning their father's funeral service by saying to me: "Let's keep the religious stuff to a minimum, Reverend. We just want to give him a good sendoff."

All ministers have stories about bizarre (and, after the fact, funny) experiences. I recall the time a funeral assistant, playing the requested recorded music, set the player at 78 rpm for a 33 rpm record and startled the mourners with a version of George Beverly Shea singing "In the Garden" that sounded like Donald Duck. I remember the woman who never forgave me for not agreeing to place a Cincinnati Reds cap over the hole where her father's ashes were to be deposited while the cemetery carillon played "Take Me Out to the Ballgame." I recall the unspeakably sad argument that turned into a full-fledged fight at the open casket between the deceased's wife and ex-wife.

Reading the articles in this issue, I realized that my own mind has changed about funeral directors. It was fashionable a few decades ago to view them as greedy purveyors of products and services that no one needs. My experience has been different. I am grateful to have known a funeral director who conducted his business with dignity and integrity, who saw his job as a ministry and who treated grieving families with compassion, patience and kindness. I have discovered that there are many like him.

I STATEMENTS: A PREACHER'S TESTIMONY

February 9, 2010

I regretted to see in the January 1 *New York Times* that Peter Steinfels was writing his final "Beliefs" column. I've rarely missed a Steinfels column over the years. They were consistently respectful and totally devoid of either simplistic advocacy or simplistic criticism. Steinfels attempted to understand and analyze the complexity of religion in contemporary America. In years when religion generally made it into the news pages only when someone did or said something outrageous, Steinfels's column was an oasis of thoughtful, theologically informed analysis. In a very brief conversation with him years ago I found him to be cordial but crisp and to the point, without hinting at all about his personal feelings on the subject we discussed—in other words, a consummate journalist.

In his last column Steinfels wrote that his choice of topics did reveal a personal perspective, but he tried to be detached. "I never wrote in the first person singular," he explained.[2]

Martin Marty picked up on that comment in his January 4 "Sightings" column and remembered that he and Dean Peerman used to coauthor a *Century* column anonymously, which occasionally led them to take refuge in "stilted phrases such as 'it seems to the present writer that.'" Some years ago the *Century* resumed an old tradition of having the lead editorial be unsigned—another case where there can be no first-person pronoun: it's an editorial that belongs to all of us.

This discussion made me think of the special place of the personal pronoun in preaching. I learned to preach at a time when there was nearly a phobia against making "I" statements. The sermon should be about the Word, not about the preacher, we were told. We delighted in poking fun at preachers who seemed always to be talking about themselves. It was good advice. It is dangerously easy for a sermon to be about the preacher's experiences, convictions, relationships, tastes, even vacations.

But I will never forget a seminar led by James Forbes in which Forbes began by saying that preaching is, among other things, testimony, and that if it is not testimony, it isn't going to work. "If you don't believe this stuff and tell them you do, why would you expect them to believe it?" That sentence hit me—it was what Forbes would call "a fax from heaven." Preaching as witness. Forbes drove the point home by asking participants to "just stand up and say what the Holy Spirit is doing in your life." I was not the only one looking for the exit.

I'm still a little skeptical and cautious about using the "I" word in sermons. I respect Steinfels's journalistic integrity and the appropriateness of other forums in which being impersonal is a virtue. But I learned from Forbes that preaching is one of those vocations where personal testimony is called for. If it is not clear that the preacher is personally committed to what he says, there is little reason to expect that anyone else will believe it.

INTERFAITH PARISHIONERS

January 21, 2011

Amy Frykholm's article "Double belonging" took me back to my first encounter with double belonging. A young man in my congregation returned from working with the Peace Corps in Vietnam. He made an appointment to see me. After describing his Peace Corps experience, including his encounters with Buddhist monks and Buddhist practice, he said, "I think I'm a Buddhist." My knowledge of Buddhism at the time, I'm ashamed to admit, was based on a 20-page chapter in a book on comparative religion.

I gently raised the question of his Christianity. "Oh," he said, "I'm still a Christian." I suggested that one could be a Buddhist or a Christian but not both. "Who says?" he asked. "Where does it say you can't be both? I haven't found anything on Buddhism that conflicts with my Christian faith or requires that I disavow my faith in Jesus Christ. In fact, there's a lot about Buddhism that feels like what real Christianity ought to be."

He continued to attend Sunday morning worship in the Presbyterian church with his family. When he fell in love he made another appointment—to discuss a wedding. His fiancée had also been brought up in a Christian church, and she too considered herself a Buddhist-Christian. She was less patient than he, wondering why I was making a big deal out of an issue that seemed simple to them. They believed that Jesus Christ was the Son of God and called people to lives of faithful following, and they also believed the best way to do that was through the practice of Buddhism.

Some of my colleagues who knew the young man and his family were sympathetic to my dilemma and to the couple's proposal. Special help came from Arthur Romig, a retired Presbyterian mission worker who served on our staff. Art was born in China of missionary parents, returned to China as a missionary, spent time in a Japanese prison camp, returned to China after World War II and served until the communist revolution. He reminded me that the issues of double belonging emerged daily in the ministry of missionaries, and that Christians had done a lot of damage to indigenous cultures when they insisted that becoming a Christian meant rejecting traditional and deeply loved cultural and religious practices.

Art's advice? Go ahead and marry the couple and see what the Spirit can do. I did, and as far as I know, they are still practicing Buddhist-Christians.

This is one of the major issues that Christian churches must deal with in the future. Some argue that we must maintain boundaries and never risk watering down Christian practices. Some argue that attending a yoga class is contrary to Christian belief and practice. (Three yoga classes meet in the church I serve, led by one of our elders.) Others, including me, hope that Christians who trust Jesus Christ as the way, the truth and the life will be open to other faith traditions and to people who find themselves compelled by and attracted to more than one of them. Every Sunday I look out at a congregation that includes several Jews, a few Muslim and Hindu guests, and a hodgepodge of skeptics, agnostics, doubters and seekers. Some of them feel at home with us, and some belong to more than one faith community.

3

In the
News

JOHN DIDN'T HAVE a lot of words per issue. He had to put a point on the issues raised in the magazine, disparate as they were every other week, and to show their center of gravity in Christ's church and the practice of ministry. We hardly stop to notice how effortlessly he did so.

In this section he looks at the news of the day—fresh and unsure from his vantage; clearer from ours, years later. The issues spring back to life with a glance at his work: guns, race, violence, war, natural disaster, the election of a pope. And I'm struck that John prayed his way through all of it. He looks prophetic in these lines. Years on we are no closer to dealing with gun violence, which has grown in our body politic like some bilious pus. His call for restrictions not on hunters, but on indiscriminate sales of assault weapons designed for death, is common sense and is still resisted by a very loud and wealthy oligarchy with a hold on our politicians' courage. When natural disasters hit, John went to his go-to move: he played librarian, suggesting books by Douglas John Hall, Nicholas Wolterstorff, and others. Here we see John at his best—not lecturing, finger-waging, "You should be reading!" but quietly demonstrating the dignity and duty of a learned clergy, implicitly inviting others to do likewise. The election of Benedict XVI had him cheering with caution, though later he would fret more. Perhaps his prayers for the new pope are answered now in the remarkable pontificate of Francis. As they say in the black church, God doesn't always come when you call, but he's always on time.

These essays have me reflecting on how we view history. The secular news can give the impression that it's just "one damn thing after another," as someone said. But no Christian can agree. History is the theater in which God displays divine glory—in the calling of Israel, in the birth of Jesus from an unmarried Jewish teenager from the sticks, in a church always on the edge of total system failure but still, stunningly, used for good by God.

I'm most impressed by John's local vantage on these international events. Katrina had him not just exploring theodicy but talking about relief work. Benedict's election reminded him of the pastor down the block at Holy Name Cathedral, recently dead as of John's writing, who whenever they were together lamented Protestant/Catholic division. In just a few words, John could render a human face, a churchly face, on events that otherwise numbingly scroll past the bottom of the cable network. It's a preacher's art. John Howard Yoder called it "viewing history doxologically." John could see that a slain lamb rules the cosmos, and his words tell the world who's in charge, despite all appearances to the contrary.

CHORDS OF REMEMBRANCE

July 28, 1999

Now that we know his flaws, not many of us can romanticize John F. Kennedy or his presidency. And the glamour of the Kennedy clan has been tarnished considerably in recent years as scholars and reporters have pointed out its members' various shortcomings.

Despite all this, the death of John F. Kennedy Jr. has struck a chord of remembrance and recognition for me, as it has for many, and it has been a cause for grief—even despite the sometimes exploitative media focus on the event. What I mourn is not only the premature death of a gifted young man, but the continuing tragedy of a family that has been a presence in our lives and the life of the nation for four decades.

And something more: As president, JFK instilled hope in a nation that was beginning to feel stale and tired. The essence of the New Frontier was the conviction that things don't have to be the way they are, things can be better for our nation—more just, more equal, more excellent, and for each of us. The name for that conviction is hope. And President Kennedy's great gift, which stands out over the less-admirable aspects of his life, was that he reawakened hope.

He did something his predecessors had difficulty accomplishing: he inspired ordinary people to want to serve their nation and their community. He spoke to something dormant in people's souls, and he made public service appealing. His vision of a world more peaceful and just may have been overly ambitious, and his domestic agenda tentative, but his efforts on behalf of civil rights were nevertheless crucial—they were the reason many of us became vocal about and involved in the civil rights movement.

The 1960 election was the first presidential election in which I voted. Along with the rest of my family, I cast my ballot for the Republican ticket. But Kennedy soon made a convert of me. His account of risk-taking politicians, *Profiles in Courage*, encouraged a generation of people to take risks for what they believed. He called many of us out of our pulpits and into our communities.

John Kennedy Jr. handled his celebrity with his father's grace. His involvement in publishing was, I always thought, a prelude to some greater involvement in public life. His death feels like a sad closure of an era, and it reminds me again of the great commitment to public life that his family has made and of the price they have paid for that commitment.

His father's famous call in his inaugural address to "ask not what your county can do for you, but what you can do for your country," sounds naive these days. It's a sentiment out of step with a culture that puts a premium on personal gain, personal success, personal fulfillment, personal gratification.

But the idea of investing one's life in the community, giving life away to the neighbor, losing one's life for the sake of one's convictions—this notion should be familiar to those who follow the one who said that to lose one's life is to find it. Such ideas are often lost in the midst of anxieties about institutional survival or church growth.

So, as the Kennedys mourn another family member whose life was cut short, I mourn with them, and at the same time feel grateful for the commitment to public service that this family helped inspire.

LEFT BEHIND

March 21, 2001

A week or so after President Bush assured the nation that education would continue to be one of his top priorities and that no child would be left behind, I had an extended conversation with the principal of an elementary school in the middle of Cabrini-Green. Cabrini is the housing project on the near north side of Chicago. Constructed in the '60s, Cabrini once housed 20,000 people. It became the symbol of everything that was misguided about public housing. It was the scene of concentrated poverty, poorly maintained buildings, unemployment, family disintegration, crime and drugs. When you take a taxi from the north side to O'Hare, the driver asks, "Division Street?" That means: "Are you willing to risk driving through Cabrini-Green?"

Many of the project's worst buildings have been torn down, and others are scheduled to come down. Some of the schools that served the project are also being replaced.

Byrd Academy is a building with about as much character as the communist-era structures of Eastern Europe. John Updike says somewhere that the old ornate school buildings which many of us attended as children reflected the community's pride, its commitment to its children, and the high premium it placed on education. I remember the high school in Altoona, Pennsylvania, with its dome visible from all over the town, and its wonderful three-story open light well. You knew when you entered the school that important activities happened inside and that the community had high expectations for you.

Byrd Academy looks like a bureaucracy's afterthought. The school has no gymnasium, no assembly area, no lunch room. Children play outside when the weather permits and eat lunch in the hallway. These kids from Cabrini and the ones who preceded them over the past four decades have already been left behind in many ways. If President Bush is serious, we have some real catching up to do.

There is a lot about Byrd Academy that is discouraging. Yet the more I talked with the principal and toured his school, the more inspired I became. In fact, Joe Gardner is my new hero, along with everyone who teaches at his school. Their commitment is palpable. Their devotion to teaching is obvious. Their love for the students is clear.

The last thing Joe Gardner showed me was a mural painted by a group of mentally challenged students. They had been asked to imagine what their neighborhood and school ought to look like. Outside the school, amid the decaying high-rise buildings, the trash was blowing about, the streets were full of potholes, and fire trucks and ambulances were regularly roaring by. But on the wall the students drew recognizable Chicago landmarks—the John Hancock Building and the Sears Towers—surrounded by lots of trees, flowers, birds, a few computers and a huge yellow butterfly.

If you want to know how far we must travel as a nation to bring all the children along, make an appointment with the principal of an urban school in a poor neighborhood. My guess is that you will be troubled but also inspired.

TO THINK AND ACT ANEW

October 10, 2001[1]

We must not expect our nation's wound to heal quickly: It is too deep and the pain is too profound. We Americans expect instant healing.

"Let's put it behind us—get over it—get on with life," we say, as if it were inappropriate to allow tragedy to be tragic for more than a day or two.

I hope we don't get over this too quickly. To do so would be to excuse ourselves from a painful but necessary period of national introspection. I do not mean to say, as some have, that we brought September 11 on ourselves, that the collective political and moral foibles of the American people resulted in us "getting what we deserved." Not at all.

But there are serious questions to be explored, such as the critical tension between security and civil liberties, and perhaps the hardest question of all: Why did those who did this do it? Their reasons may be misguided, immoral, evil and insane, but it is irresponsible not to probe and study and ask and listen until we know the reasons. One of our readers wrote us that his daughter asked, "Daddy, why do they hate us?" Why indeed? Those responsible seemed to be well-educated, mature husbands and fathers. Why were they willing to die to hurt us?

Of course, the fault is not ours. But we do need to find out what it is about us that stimulates and feeds this hatred. Personally, I'm glad to know that we have appropriated funds and deployed aircraft carriers. I'm grateful for President Bush's resolve not to tolerate this terrorism. But I also hope and pray for the moral courage and stamina to lead the nation in a reexamination of the role we play in the new global environment. What we do or do not do reverberates across nations and cultures in ways we do not intend, but must now understand.

Pulitzer Prize-winning author David Kennedy observed in the *New York Times* that the terrorist attack cannot be "countered simply by mustering the nation's prodigious human, financial and industrial brawn" as we did in World War II.[2] "Against our new foes our conventional arsenal is all but useless." Kennedy then quotes words from Abraham Lincoln's second inaugural address, given on December 1, 1862, a bleak moment in American history. I've always thought that this address includes some of the most important words any American ever spoke:

> "The dogmas of the quiet past are inadequate to the stormy present. The occasion is piled high with difficulty and we must rise with the occasion. As our case is new, so we must think anew, and act anew. We must disenthrall ourselves, and then we shall save our country."

Let's pray to God for the moral courage to think anew and act anew in the perilous days ahead.

GUN PLAY

May 17, 2003

As bombs were dropping in Baghdad, the U.S. Supreme Court took up the question of whether it is legitimate to consider racial identity in setting university admission policies. Meanwhile, Congress debated the budget, including an unprecedented tax cut. Largely unnoticed was the passage by the House of Representatives of the Protection of Lawful Commerce in Arms Act, which exempts the makers, distributors and sellers of guns from liability for gun violence.

This bill is a response to some 30 lawsuits that have been filed against the gun industry by municipalities, including Chicago, New York, Cleveland and Detroit. Given the absence of decisive legislation on the issue, such lawsuits offer an important way to try to curb the spread of guns.

Though the issue of gun violence in our homes, streets and schools seems to have disappeared from the headlines, it hit me with a jolt during Holy Week. First I read about a murder in a crowded high school gym in New Orleans. Four young men entered the gym and shot 15-year-old Jonathan Williams with an AK-47. A .45-caliber pistol was found in Williams's pocket. Why don't we seem to be concerned that an AK-47, a military assault-type weapon, is in the hands of teenagers, not to mention the .45 in the dead youth's pocket?

Then I read about a how six-year-old Chicago boy was playing with a loaded handgun in his grandparents' home and fatally shot himself.

Later in the week I learned that a classmate of my 12-year-old grandson had gone to the restroom, pulled a gun out of her backpack and killed herself. I couldn't believe what I was hearing.

Then in late April I read about how a 14-year-old in Pennsylvania shot his principal and then turned a gun on himself.

Events like this are happening not only every day, but eight times a day. In 2000, 3,042 children and teenagers were killed by guns; 1,806 were homicides, 1,007 suicides and 229 accidents. Every day five children are murdered and three commit suicide with guns. There were 28,663 gun-related deaths in 2000. Firearms have killed more than 28,000 Americans every year since 1972.

I have heard all the arguments against gun control. I am not talking here about interfering with hunters or target shooters. I am talking about a society that is inundated by guns. A revived public discussion is

needed. (A good resource is the HELP Network—at www.helpnetwork
.org—an organization my congregation supports.) Many politicians
won't touch the issue because of the power of the gun lobby. It's time
for the rest of us to speak up.

WHEN IN ROME: HOPES FOR BENEDICT XVI

May 17, 2005

It was fascinating to be in Rome on the day Pope John Paul II died
and to be in Italy as the College of Cardinals elected Cardinal Joseph
Ratzinger to be the new head of the Roman Catholic Church.

I used the occasion to meet with a good friend, Father John Radano,
an American on the staff of the Pontifical Council for Promoting Christian Unity. Father Radano and I became acquainted when I visited the
Vatican as a representative of the Presbyterian Church (U.S.A.) and
when I took part in a series of Presbyterian-Catholic dialogues. He is a
distinguished scholar and an experienced church diplomat. We had a
good conversation and dinner at one of his favorite restaurants near St.
Peter's. I was impressed again with how seriously the Vatican takes ecumenical and interfaith relationships and how far the Catholic Church
has come since the papacy of John XXIII.

It is always stunning, of course, for an American Protestant to visit
St. Peter's and take in Michelangelo's dome, his heroic Sistine Chapel
and his Pietá; Bernini's columns reaching out like a mother's arms to
embrace the world; and the bright colors of robes, banners, flags and
uniforms, accented against the gray white massiveness of the basilica.
One can't help being struck by the historical impact of the Vatican.
The surroundings tell you: this is an important enterprise. The scene
also evokes from me a quiet prayer of thanksgiving for Martin Luther
and John Calvin, who inspired an alternative way of thinking about
church and whose heirs are responsible for sustaining a respectful, honest tension with Rome and our Roman Catholic friends.

Protestants my age can recall what seemed to be the cold, distant
person of Pius XII. Those who know history have very serious concerns
about his role during World War II. We can also recall the euphoria we
experienced when John XXIII opened the windows of the church and

allowed the winds of the spirit to blow. Many of us had mixed feelings about John Paul II. There was much to like about the man: his energy, wit and courage, and the way his pastoral presence touched millions of people, from dock workers in Poland to politicians to children and families around the world. In his dying he gave a courageous witness, living out his sense of God's call to his last breath.

He apologized to Judaism for anti-Semitism—something my own church has yet to do. He prayed at the Western Wall. He told President Bush that he didn't agree with the U.S. invasion of Iraq. During his papacy the church talked to ecumenical partners and representatives of other faiths.

At the same time, John Paul II held the line on many of the issues that separate Catholics and Protestants: birth control; the use of condoms to prevent disease and AIDS; the role of women; clerical celibacy. He treated clergy sexual abuse of children as if it were an American problem and rewarded Cardinal Bernard Law—who overlooked abuse and reassigned abusing priests in Boston—with a soft job and comfortable apartment in Rome. Protestants are cautiously hopeful about Benedict XVI, who served as John Paul's theological right hand man as prefect of the Congregation for the Doctrine of Faith. Many Protestants were stunned by the congregation's 2000 statement, *Dominus Iesus*. It reaffirmed the Catholic Church's view that there "exists a single church of Christ, which subsists in the Catholic Church, governed by the Successor of Peter," and it termed other church bodies to be "not churches in the proper sense." This sounded like a return to the spirit of pre-Vatican II Catholicism.

Several days before his election, Cardinal Ratzinger made a speech attacking the "dictatorship of relativism, liberalism, radical individualism and the creation of 'sects,'" a term the Vatican used to employ to describe Protestant churches. In his first public statement as Benedict XVI, however, he struck an altogether different note. He spoke about the importance of unity, not only among Roman Catholics, but with other Christian churches. He expressed respect and regard for other religions and used the word "dialogue" four times. Around Italy there was an almost audible sigh of relief as Benedict, who chose the name of the revered author of the Benedictine Rule—someone known more for pastoral listening than pontificating—distanced himself from his image as Catholicism's theological enforcer.

Benedict XVI has work to do. His church has a major leadership crisis. The shortage of priests in Europe and North America is a huge problem, and Catholics in those regions virtually ignore Catholic teaching on birth control and abortion. In Europe, few attend mass. The pope needs to respond faithfully and creatively to the 21st century. I hope he will find ways to do so other than returning to the past.

As I observed all of this I found myself thinking about one of the best friends I ever had, Father Bob McLaughlin, pastor of Holy Name Cathedral in Chicago. We worked together, enjoyed one another's company, shared a love for the Cubs, and brought our congregations together in mission and worship. After 9/11, on an occasion when we led a joint worship service and Bob preached from a Presbyterian pulpit, he said, "John, when we are together I feel the pain of our separation deeply." Bob died, unexpectedly, two months ago. My prayer is that something of his spirit will live in the papacy of Benedict XVI.

KATRINA: HOW TO RESPOND TO TRAGEDY?

October 4, 2005

For the second time in ten months our attention has been commanded by a natural catastrophe—there was the tsunami this past December in Southeast Asia and now Hurricane Katrina on the Gulf Coast. As I write, Hurricane Ophelia is bearing down on the North Carolina coast, where my family has vacationed for decades.

Church response to Katrina has been strong and helpful: offerings directed to relief services on the ground, efforts at resettling displaced people, and lots of hands-on aid. The congregation I serve teamed up with Holy Name Cathedral and within a few hours filled a semitruck with diapers, peanut butter and granola bars to send to victims.

Meanwhile, there is pastoral and hermeneutical work to be done. There is nothing more distressing to the human spirit than the suggestion that in the final analysis nature cannot be trusted, and that if the creator God is involved in the natural world, it is not apparent how.

In this issue Walter Brueggemann points out that there is no one teaching on the meaning of natural disasters in the Bible and that a generously biblical approach will at least acknowledge four dimensions of the topic, from the prophetic to the pastoral. (See "A Disaster of 'Biblical' Proportions.") Our trust that "God finally prevails over chaos to sustain life and keep it safe" does not mean that suffering and death will not happen to innocent human beings, as every pastor regularly witnesses. It means that, from a Christian perspective, there is a dynamic going on in and through even the most horrific suffering that will finally be redemptive.

Canadian theologian Douglas John Hall writes: "God's problem is not that God can't do certain things. God's problem is that God loves! Love complicates the life of God as it complicates every human life" (*God and Human Suffering*).

As I was pondering all of this I witnessed another way that love complicates our lives but also redeems them. I watched as my daughter and her husband took their daughter to college. It is an old drama. These parents love their firstborn so much that they are going to do a most extraordinary thing: they are going to let her go. They will take her to college in another state, they will help her settle in, maybe even make her bed for the first time, and then they will get in the car and drive away, leaving her alone. But she won't really be alone. Their love will remain with her. In time she will understand that their leaving her was not abandonment, but the full expression of their love.

They are experiencing a deep theological truth even though they may not name it. The finest thing love can do is give the gift of freedom. It is not without pain, nor is it without risk. But genuine love lets go, backs away, gets in the car and drives off, and allows a beloved child the freedom necessary for her authentic personhood, with all the risk that entails.

There may be a prophetic word to be spoken about Katrina, but from my perspective it is not about the sinfulness of Mardi Gras or about God's wrathful judgment on the sins of the flesh. Rather, the prophetic word concerns the human refusal to be responsible about the environment and global warming; it concerns the human engineering that violates nature's wisdom about rivers and deltas; and it targets the political insensitivity that issues evacuation orders to a population one quarter of which has no way to evacuate, and then essentially abandons them.

ENERGIZED: THE FACES OF THE YOUNG PEOPLE

December 2, 2008

Whatever else you might think about the outcome of the election, Barack Obama energized young adults in a way that was reminiscent of John F. Kennedy's campaign.

As I watched the election returns and the wonderfully diverse crowd that gathered in Chicago's Grant Park to celebrate Obama's victory, I remembered my own first exposure to the civil rights movement and how the connection between Christian faith and the quest for racial justice caught my imagination and solidified my sense of call to ministry.

I remembered hearing a young guest preacher from Atlanta by the name of Martin Luther King Jr. in Rockefeller Chapel at the University of Chicago. I remembered Andrew Young visiting the school and telling us that some ministers needed to get involved in demonstrations and marches in the South—and that the rest needed to stay home to explain what was happening to their white congregations.

I remembered marching in downtown Lafayette, Indiana, after Martin Luther King was assassinated and signing a petition advocating the formation of a human rights commission—and getting in hot water with some of my congregation when I wrote a letter to the commission, published in the local newspaper, asking the city to remove a black-faced post boy standing by a hitching post in front of a prominent fire station.

As the votes were tallied and Obama's victory became evident, television cameras showed the reaction of crowds of Republican and Democratic supporters. There was sadness on the losing side, but not much anger that I could see. In conceding the election, John McCain could not have been more gracious and honorable as he pledged his support for the new president. It was a time to be grateful for a country practiced in the peaceful transfer of power.

In the end, though, it was the faces of the young people that stayed with me. I thought of Thomas Friedman's comment in his book *Hot, Flat and Crowded*: "Our young people are so much more idealistic than we deserve them to be, . . . still eager to be enlisted—to fix education, research renewable energy, repair our infrastructure, help others. They want our country to matter again, they want to be summoned . . . to some great project worthy of America . . . to nation-building not just in Iraq and Afghanistan, but nation-building in America."

COMPROMISE

January 12, 2010

By the time this issue of the magazine is in your hands, the fate of health-care reform may have been decided by Congress. The legislative process, like the proverbial production of sausage, is not neat or pretty. If a bill passes, it will not be all the Obama administration hoped for and it will be a lot more than the Republican opposition wants.

Churchpeople have had a devilish time trying to reach a compromise on controversial issues such as whether gays and lesbians may be ordained ministers. For many there seems to be little if any room for maneuvering. The Presbyterian Church (U.S.A.) spent two years coming up with a Peace, Unity and Purity policy that would allow some individuals and governing bodies the possibility of diverging from national policies. I hoped that it would offer a way to live together with our different views, but it appears not to be working. Each side is gearing up for another battle on the provisions. Many people think it is time to acknowledge our conflicts as irresolvable and divide into two smaller, more ideologically pure bodies. Division is the way our church has resolved conflicts in the past. Presbyterians have made schism an art form.

Schism is not an option for Congress. It took a very bloody civil war and a half million deaths to make that point in the 1860s. So the process of health-care reform will stumble and lurch along.

In *The New Yorker* (Dec. 7, "Preexisting Condition") Jill Lepore quoted Yale economist Irving Fisher: "At present the United States has the unenviable distinction of being the only great industrial nation without compulsory health insurance." Fisher made that remark in 1916.

Lepore also quoted Congresswoman Shirley Jackson-Lee, who observed that it was funny to call this current effort at reform "rushed." "America has been working on providing access to health care for all

Americans since the nineteen-thirties, forties, fifties, sixties, seventies, eighties, and . . . nineties." And, the nineteen-tens.

Health care for all is an issue of justice. It is part of the peace, security and wholeness—the shalom—that the Bible tells us is a sign of the reign of God. If a health-care reform bill passes, it will mean that some deeply convicted men and women found a way to compromise. Could it be that a bit of God's kingdom would be realized via the art of compromise? If so, maybe churches should be paying attention.

SCORCHED EARTH

December 19, 2011

How is it possible to read the first chapter of the Bible and not be an environmentalist? The stunning and unique affirmations of Genesis 1 point to a creation that is good, one that reflects the being and will of God. The first and primary human moral obligation is to take care of the place. How can people who believe that the Bible is or contains the word of God ignore this directive?

In the U.S., it is a particularly dicey time for those concerned about the environment given the fractured political atmosphere and the absence of rational discourse in the primary election campaign. Sandra Steingraber presses to revive the conversation. In an interview ("How we're poisoning our children"), she discusses the environmental crisis we are in and puts it in ethical context. She invokes one of my personal heroes, Presbyterian minister and newspaper publisher Elijah Lovejoy, who opposed slavery and was killed in a proslavery riot in the 1830s.

Steingraber calls President Obama's recent override of EPA protections against smog pollution the worst decision the administration has made. Smog leads to ozone, she reminds us, and "ozone kills people—elders and infants disproportionately." The dilemma is that our economy has become dependent on ruinously destructive practices. Steingraber calls our dependency on fossil fuels a "homicidal abomination."

So why aren't we talking about this? Why have global warming and environmental concerns disappeared from the political agendas of both parties? In the October 15 *New York Times,* reporter Elisabeth Rosenthal observed that as recently as the 2008 presidential election, both candidates John McCain and Barack Obama warned about human-influenced global warming and publicly supported legislation to curb emissions.[3] Only the U.S., says Rosenthal, has stopped talking about it. Europe has always been ahead of us on this issue, and emerging economies like those of India, China and Brazil are pursuing "aggressive climate politics."

But in the United States, says Rosenthal, the issue has been hijacked by powerful right-wing leaders who have made "skepticism about man-made global warming into a requirement for electability, forming an unlikely triad with antiabortion and gun-rights beliefs."

I am disappointed that the president overrode the EPA on emissions. I am also disappointed that ideologically driven politicians have transformed an issue that has everything to do with our future into a political litmus test, so that no one in either party can risk talking about it.

We could let the discouraging reality of the environmental crisis lead us to despair. But Steingraber calls this despair the "biggest obstacle to social and environmental justice."

Instead, in such a time as this, we need more activists like Steingraber, those who firmly refuse to lose hope and who believe that people of good will and reasonable intelligence can act to pull us out of this crisis and ensure a viable future for our grandchildren.

TORTURED ENDS AND MEANS

January 5, 2015

Philosophers and ethicists have long pondered whether a good and noble end justifies any means of attaining it. The age-old debate has come up again with the release of the Senate Intelligence Committee's report on CIA detention activities following the attacks of September 11, 2001. Consequentialists (like Jeremy Bentham, John Stuart Mill, and currently Sam Harris and Peter Singer) would argue that good outcomes justify the means employed to accomplish them. President Harry Truman reasoned that dropping atomic bombs on Japanese cities, killing hundreds of thousands of civilians, was justified because it avoided an even more ghastly loss of life in an American invasion of Japan.

On the other hand, deontologists conclude that the morality of an act derives from the act itself rather than the outcome. They are certain that killing or torturing people is always wrong even if it saves many more innocent lives.

Thirteen years after 9/11, we are discovering and pondering the details of the methods our government employed to track down the people who attacked us, their support networks, and those organizations and individuals who make no secret of their intent to harm Americans.

In the 1930s and '40s, Reinhold Niebuhr broke with Social Gospel and pacifist academics and journalists, including the editor of this magazine, because he believed that it was morally irresponsible not to respond with force to the rising fascist movements in Germany, Italy, and Japan. Moral responsibility requires resisting evil, Niebuhr reasoned. I find that argument compelling. And I'm grateful for our armed forces and intelligence agencies and the men and women who devote their lives to our security.

That said, I can't agree that torturing a human being is justified if it produces greater national security. For one thing, the value and sanctity of human life is at the heart of our national ethics—and of Christian faith. This nation grew out of the conviction that individuals are endowed with unalienable rights. Although we are still struggling to live into that radical notion, it remains at the very center of who we are as a people. It is our core value.

In addition, Niebuhrian realists would acknowledge that torture does not produce reliable information. Torture sometimes works in the opposite way as victims of sustained physical pain may say whatever their torturers want to hear in order to stop the agony.

The United States military understands that fact and forbids torture, not only because it invites an enemy to reciprocate and endangers the lives of American soldiers who are captured, but also because the information gained is not always accurate or useful.

Senator John McCain is one national figure who argues against the use of torture. McCain's position on torture is grounded in his own experience as a POW. He was subjected to years of torture at the hands of his North Vietnamese captors. McCain says torture doesn't work and is always wrong. I agree.

POLICE ENCOUNTERS

January 23, 2015

When I was in elementary school a local police officer made regular visits to explain to us what police did. The department always sent Sergeant Cal Bell, a genial African American who showed us the exotic equipment he carried: badge, large flashlight, nightstick, handcuffs, and service revolver. He told us that he liked to be called "Cow Bell," which we kids thought was hilarious. I asked him if he had ever used his revolver. "No," he said, "I have never shot it in the line of duty, and I hope I never have to."

When I was 12, police in an unmarked car stopped a friend and me one evening when we were spraying passing automobiles with our new squirt guns. They confiscated our water pistols, drove us to our homes, hauled us up the front steps, and turned us over to our parents.

My adult encounters with the police include a few traffic tickets, one of which was received while I was wearing a clerical collar. I assumed that the collar would inspire sympathy—it didn't. Then a few years ago I had a flat tire on my bicycle while riding on Chicago's lakefront bike path. Two police officers, a young woman and young man patrolling on bicycles, rode up as I was trying, unsuccessfully, to repair my tire. I asked if they could help me return home. "We'll do better than that," one said, and they removed the wheel, applied a quick patch, and reinflated the tire. I was grateful.

In years of ministry in city churches I always made a point of becoming familiar with the local police station and acquainted with the commanding officer. In Columbus, Ohio, a clinical psychologist who worked with the metropolitan police force told me that police officers are susceptible not only to daily physical danger but also to psychological stress. Being called to intervene in and defuse a domestic conflict, for instance, exacts a toll. The average urban cop, my friend said, experiences the fight-or-flight physical and emotional response several times every day and pays a steep price in stress levels and health.

I am distressed by the recent police shooting and killing of unarmed civilians and, in one incident, the death of a man by an illegal choke hold. In each incident the victim was African American, including a 12-year-old boy brandishing a BB gun (the age I was when police confiscated my water pistol).

Those of us who are white have had to recognize that African-American communities experience and perceive the police differently and are treated differently by the police. While my experience confirms the comforting Chicago police motto, "To Serve and Protect," many blacks in Chicago likely don't see it that way at all.

One picture from Ferguson, Missouri, captures the enormous gap in perception. An African-American man in jeans, T-shirt, and backward baseball cap raises his arms in the "don't shoot" gesture as he backs away from three law enforcement officers in full paramilitary gear. Their automatic weapons are pointed directly at the retreating black man.

Prominent right-wing politicians are attempting to deepen the conflict by blaming the victims. Some police union officers are arguing that there is widespread hostility toward police in general, which there most certainly is not.

Our country needs a national conversation between police and the communities they serve, with an acknowledgment of past inequities, a renewed appreciation for those who serve and protect, and a renewed commitment on the part of the judicial system, including law enforcement, to ensuring that skin color has nothing to do with the way citizens are treated.

A DIFFERENT KIND OF POWER

July 6, 2015

The shooting of the innocent happens regularly in this country. But what happened at Charleston's Emanuel African Methodist Episcopal Church feels uniquely evil. Nine African Americans attending a Wednesday evening prayer meeting were systematically executed by a 20-year-old white man.

Why would anyone do such a thing? President Obama sounded weary and resigned as he reminded us, once again, that "every country has violent, hateful, or mentally unstable people," but only the United States allows easy access to guns. There have been 14 mass killings during his presidency, but President Obama's effort to galvanize public opinion after the Sandy Hook school killings in Newtown, Connecticut, produced nothing but a national yawn, and Senate efforts to come up with meaningful gun controls produced absolutely nothing.

What is it about us that is causing the unthinkable to happen regularly? Why are so many white males so obsessed with guns and gun ownership that lawmakers are allowing them to buy, carry, and display firearms almost everywhere? Some suggest that in this time of economic turmoil, male self-esteem is the issue. Yet we survived the Great Depression and massive unemployment without anything like this kind of violence.

There are too many guns in our nation—300 million of them. This plethora of firearms, along with a latent racism brought to the surface by the election of a black president, and paranoia about governmental authority generate a lethal condition. The National Rifle Association exploits people's fears by translating the constitutional right to bear arms into a political defiance requiring heroic determination and commitment.

Ninety percent of the American people are in favor of gun control: thorough background checks, digital records that law enforcement agencies can share, prohibition of multiple gun purchases. Yet state legislatures are making it easier to acquire and carry a firearm. The Texas state legislature recently voted to allow open carry of firearms on college and university campuses—one of the worst ideas ever.

It is time for a renaissance of common sense and political courage. Senators, congressional representatives, and state legislators must somehow summon the courage and political will to defy the power of the gun lobby and respond to their constituents who want meaningful gun control.

In the meantime we are blessed by the Christian witness of the nine Charleston martyrs and a Christian community that is teaching the power, not of guns, but of vulnerable love. Pat Buchanan has suggested that the tragedy would have been averted if Pastor Clementa Pinckney had been carrying a gun and had shot the killer. The victims' families and the people of Mother Emmanuel are showing us a different kind of power—the power of forgiveness and love, which is to say the power of the cross.

4
War and
Peace

IT IS SOMETIMES SAID that for the right, every U.S. military engagement is World War II. For the left, they are all Vietnam. Both mythologies are important. World War II: a Manichean struggle between the forces of darkness and the forces of light that no morally sound person could absent her- or himself from. Vietnam: a quagmire where right and wrong are indistinguishable and any morally sound person should stay at home (or move to Canada).

The *Christian Century* had its most famous public spat over the question of war during the run up to World War II. C. C. Morrison abided by the magazine's longtime pacifist stance, and favorite son Reinhold Niebuhr left to found *Christianity and Crisis* to advocate responding more forcefully to totalitarianism. That journal lasted until the early 1990s, and after World War II, it found few wars it liked (to its credit). Its demise points to the extraordinary ongoing existence of the *Century* long after similar journals have vanished.

John Buchanan's own position on war and peace is closer to Niebuhr's realism than Morrison's social gospel pacifism: you see here grudging support for state violence in the first Gulf War and in Afghanistan, and a brave wish for a pause in the Bush-inspired rush up to the unnecessary war in Iraq in 2003. Buchanan the pastor is also on display in the record of respectful engagement with military chaplains and academies. Those who actually *talk* to military people find not the bloodlust of much armchair pacifist imagination, but quite morally serious people willing to die for their country and preferring not to kill for it. You also find here wise reflections on the new American empire. Is this what we really want? Andrew Bacevich notes that the United States once demilitarized after conflicts. After World War II we never did. It's not surprising, then, that we go around using that gloriously funded and patriotically supported army with clockwork regularity. The result is real, human cost—Bacevich's son died leading troops in Iraq. Buchanan asks a question that's become rank heresy in some of the United States: Do we really need to run the world with our arms?

Perhaps someone else is already ruling the world in a different way.

The church is already participant in a kingdom that runs on different rules than the empires that rule here. That kingdom breaks in at unpredictable and breathtaking times and places—like in the troubles in Northern Ireland, a podium at West Point, or even the trenches of World War I.

IN A FOREIGN PLACE

November 21, 2001

It's a cliche to observe that since September 11 we are living in a different world, that everything seems different now. But it is true. I heard Harvard's Peter Gomes say recently that things sound different now. Phrases read and spoken for thousands of years suddenly sound immediate, as if they were written last week for us. The weekly reading of the Psalter in worship, an experience that for many people is simply endured, and doesn't offer much intellectual engagement, suddenly became very relevant, according to one regular worshiper at Harvard's Memorial Church. That's been my experience as well.

"The Lord is my shepherd . . . even though I walk through the valley of the shadow of death, I will fear no evil . . ." "Out of the depths I cry to you, O Lord. Lord hear my voice! . . . By the rivers of Babylon— there we sat down and wept . . . How could we sing the Lord's song in a foreign land?" As I read those words now, I hear them differently. They feel as if they have been written for us, in this new world—this foreign place.

I have pondered particularly the words of Jesus about loving enemies and what they have to do with the war President Bush has declared on terrorism and the bombs the U.S. is dropping on Afghanistan. I am not troubled by American resolve to apprehend those who orchestrated, supported, funded and carried out the attacks on September 11. But I am troubled by the fact that the people of Afghanistan, arguably among the poorest, most oppressed and most long-suffering on the face of the earth, are the ones absorbing the fury of our war on terrorism.

I am concerned that we are dropping food parcels in Afghanistan and asking school children to donate dollars to help feed hungry Afghanistan children, after years of looking the other way as Afghanistan descended into political and economic chaos. And I am deeply worried that what we are doing is fueling the very rage in the Islamic world that produced Osama bin Laden and his supporters in the first place.

And I confess that, given everything that is going on, and the cycle of violence from which there seems to be no escape, I think Jesus was not a dreamy idealist but a supreme realist when he told his surprised disciples, and us, to love our enemies.

TIME OUT: GRIEVING, NOT RETALIATING, MAY BE THE BEST ROAD TO PEACE

August 14, 2002

I am probably not alone in deploring both the suicide bombings carried out by young Palestinians against pathetically vulnerable Israeli civilians and the now predictable military attacks by Israel carried out against pathetically vulnerable Palestinian civilians. The placing of bombs in crowded marketplaces, on buses and in restaurants, and the strategic targeting of the people who plan the bombings and train the bombers—both activities result in tragic and innocent civilian deaths.

I am probably not alone in understanding that while there are occasions when a strong and efficient military response is necessary, the risks that go along with every military action are enormous and unpredictable. For what it's worth, I think the gulf war was a tragedy, but a necessary tragedy.

I know I am not alone in hoping and praying for the security of Israel and also for the creation of a viable and secure Palestinian nation. And I know I am not alone in desperately wishing my own government would play a more helpful and creative role and not appear to be so one-sided.

Moral clarity about what is transpiring in Jerusalem and Ramallah these days is hard to come by. Perhaps moral unease is the only proper posture.

This issue offers some resources for exploring that unease. David Gushee ("Just War Divide") gives a fresh exegesis of "just war" doctrine, and a reminder of our unique context, unwelcome as it may be: "When we Americans talk about war and justice, we're not Swedes or Malaysians." John Kelsay ("Suicide Bombers") also pursues the issue of justice in warfare, underscoring the importance of proportionality and discrimination, and he helps us understand, even if we don't want to, how suicide bombers seem like martyrs to many in the Muslim world. In a related article, George Hunsinger ("Iraq: Don't Go There") explores the momentum that has been generated in Washington behind a war with Iraq, and he reminds us how precarious and costly that enterprise would be.

Peacemaking requires the very best of us. It requires a strong military and the willingness to use it. But it also requires tenacity, courage and hope. My personal prayer is that Israel will not respond militarily to the next attack but instead will say something like this: "To honor our innocent victims, to consecrate the precious lives of our young people who have died, we will not respond by killing your innocent civilians. This time we will do nothing but grieve—and we invite you to join us in our grief."

Military types will laugh at the naivete and weakness of that response. But I sense that I am not at all alone in concluding that it is perhaps the only realistically hopeful response left.

NATIONAL INTERESTS: MORAL STRENGTH

March 8, 2003

What kind of country are we, and what kind of country do we wish to be? Robert Bellah has asked that question many times and in many ways over the years. In *Habits of the Heart* he explored the American culture of individualism, and he sought to revive a tradition of citizenship and concern for the public good. In *The Broken Covenant* he examined the civil religion that has shaped, positively and negatively, American values and public life.

In this issue, Bellah considers the emergence of an American empire. As some political leaders are consciously seeking to define a new, imperial role for this country, Bellah asks again: What kind of country are we, and what kind of country do we wish to be? Is the U.S. really ready to assume the tasks of empire? What cultural resources will we draw on to sustain an empire? What kind of influence do we want to have on the world? Since September 11, we have also faced this question: what defensive measures are needed to protect ourselves and our children from people who wish to do harm to America? The immediate crisis facing the nation and the international community is over whether to launch a war with Iraq in an effort to disarm that country. Is such a war necessary to ensure our safety?

Those are important, unavoidable questions, and they relate directly, of course, to questions of empire. The articles in this issue by Bellah, Theodore Weber and Gary Dorrien direct us back to the larger set of questions which provide the context for dealing with the present crisis: What kind of nation do we want to be? How should our unquestioned military and economic dominance be used? Is a "unipolar" world, one in which the U.S. is the unchallenged power, really a more secure world? Is the vision of a Pax Americana, of a world remade through American force—a vision now touted in the highest circles of government—realistic or desirable? These have become decisive strategic and political questions, and they need to be debated.

At this point, I know I want my country to be as morally great as it is economically and militarily. And I want my country to be a responsible partner in the family of nations and to support, not ignore and undermine, international agreements and the United Nations itself.

And as for the Iraq crisis: I don't want my nation to go to war unless it is absolutely necessary and only after we have exhausted every other possible solution. I don't think we are there yet.

CONGREGATION IN UNIFORM: UNSELECTIVE SERVICE

June 14, 2003

We've received a small but steady stream of letters objecting to the advertisements in our pages for military chaplaincy. Some have argued that military chaplaincy is objectionable on moral grounds and probably unconstitutional. Others have been distressed by the way the chaplain in the ads seems to be blessing military activity. Some accused us of caving in to the culture of war and concluded that we'd probably advertise anything so long as the customer paid the price.

The magazine's editors are not of one mind on this issue, and such diversity is probably a pretty good thing in a journal like this one. As we discussed the issue, I recalled a phone conversation I had with a chaplain at West Point during the Vietnam War. He had inquired if I might be interested in applying for one of the assistant chaplain positions at the academy.

The massacre at My Lai had just occurred, and after a long struggle I had concluded that the U.S. presence and activity in Southeast Asia was wrong and that I needed to go public with my convictions. I wrote the chaplain a long and what I intended to be thoughtful letter, declining his offer and explaining why I thought the war was wrong.

A few days later I was told there was a man on the phone who said he was from West Point and he sounded angry. "Buchanan," he said when I answered, "I don't like this [expletive deleted] war either. But that doesn't mean I have the right to back away from some of the finest young Americans at the very time their needs are the greatest."

"Who do you think you are?" he asked. "You've just decided not to be a minister to the brightest and best of our young people, the ones who will go on to become national leaders in the military, education, science, politics, at the very moment in their lives when their values are being formed. I hope you feel good about that." Then he hung up.

When I had the privilege of serving the Presbyterian Church (U.S.A.) as moderator of the General Assembly I visited some of our chaplains and found them committed to their sense of call, aware of the constitutional and theological issues accompanying military chaplaincy and willing to live with the tensions because of their commitment to their flocks. They also felt distant from their church.

I talked to a Korean Presbyterian woman serving as an army chaplain who told me about wading ashore in Haiti with her unit in the middle of the night, unarmed, not knowing what she would encounter. I talked to a navy chaplain, near retirement, who went with his marine unit yearly to Okinawa to spend several months living in a tent, in tropical heat, fighting sand fleas and counseling young marines separated for six months from families, spouses and children.

Christians are involved in this world. Being a faithful Christian means risking getting one's hands dirty. I've learned to respect those who minister to people in the military, even if I may disagree with what the military is doing. The actions of the military, and the role of chaplains, are issues we will continue to address in the content of the magazine. And we'll continue to run ads for military chaplaincy.

SAFE SPACES: A PLACE FOR DIALOGUE AND FORGIVENESS

June 27, 2006

In times of crisis, churches rise to the occasion. Rich Preheim's article ("Storms and Stress") about ministry on the Gulf Coast makes me proud of the often-maligned institutional church, which has poured dollars and volunteers into the disaster-struck areas. Ronald Wells's article on reconciliation in Northern Ireland ("Facing Truth") shows us the church, in the person of Desmond Tutu, engaged in a difficult but critical witness for peace and reconciliation. Peacemaking requires patience, forbearance, determination and vulnerability. It can also get you in trouble and occasionally in danger.

Wells mentions that there are communities in Northern Ireland that provide "safe space for dialogue and forgiveness," such as the Corrymeela Community in Ballycastle. It is an ecumenical peace community that grew out of Coventry Cathedral's Cross of Nails Fellowship.

I once took a group of teenagers to Corrymeela to meet with Irish teenagers, Protestant and Catholic. The kids got along wonderfully. They soon moved beyond issues of peace and violence—which the Irish youngsters were candid about and the American teenagers stunned by—to talk about pressing issues like rock music.

At the time, Corrymeela was hosting a group called Belfast Mums—wives of operatives in the Irish Republican Army who were being held in the British prison of Long Kesh. One of the most prominent of those prisoners, Bobby Sands, had just died at the end of a long hunger strike. His picture was everywhere in Belfast and Ballycastle. Corrymeela had invited the Mums and their children to have a small holiday near the ocean, away from the crowded tenements. Every evening, after their children were in bed, they gathered to talk. I got to sit in one evening.

The conversation began awkwardly at first. But then one of the Mums pulled out a bottle and passed it around the circle. Then they started talking about their husbands, the violence in which they lived, the hatred they experienced from the Protestants and the hatred they felt in return. The bottle continued to be passed. "Let's sing one for Bobby," one of them said, and they sang a lament for their husbands, their children, their hopes for peace. I learned then that peacemaking means being patient and quiet, listening and sometimes "singing one for Bobby."

TALKING POINTS: READING SCRIPTURE TOGETHER ACROSS THE BOUNDARIES OF FAITH

September 5, 2006

During the first Iraq war, after the United States started dropping bombs as a prelude to Desert Storm, homiletics professor David Buttrick surveyed mainline churches around the country to see if the war had been mentioned on the previous Sunday, whether in the sermon or in the voicing of prayers and concerns. In the vast majority of cases the answer was no.

Granted, some social and geopolitical issues are so large and so complicated that the preacher is not sure what to say.

When I find myself in this situation, knowing that people are coming to worship with such serious matters on their hearts and minds, but knowing too that I don't have a clear word from the Lord on the matter, I say something like this: "Bombs are falling, our nation is at war, precious lives are being lost, and the situation is so complicated that people of good will come to different conclusions about it. Let's hold all of that up to God—the violence, the killing and dying, and our own fears, hopes and confusion." So it was as Christians pondered the war in Lebanon. A fragile cease-fire seems to be holding, but it may have been broken down by the time you read this. While Israel had every right to respond to Hezbollah's incursion on its border, the Israeli response in bombing civilian areas believed to harbor Hezbollah operatives and rocket launching sites caused many civilian deaths. It also created greater support for Hezbollah in Lebanon and throughout the Middle East and deepened hostility toward Israel and the United States. The war promises to create more violence in the future.

I have good and respected friends who differ vehemently about this issue. Some—and I'm inclined to agree—point to Israel's occupation of Palestine as fundamentally wrong and ultimately counterproductive,

and see Israel's strong military response to Hezbollah as disproportion-
ate and counterproductive. Other friends, particularly Jewish friends,
see Israel's existence at stake and believe that a strong military response
is necessary for Israel to survive. I can understand that view too.

One of the things we all can do is keep talking to one another:
Christians, Jews and Muslims. That's why Jeffrey Bailey's article,
"Sacred Book Club," on scriptural reasoning—the practice of reading
scripture together across the boundaries of religion—gives me hope.
The other thing we can do is hold all of our hopes and fears up to the
God of Abraham and Sarah, whose will is shalom, for and among all
God's children.

TRUE PATRIOT: A VOICE OF REASON
AND COMMON SENSE

January 23, 2007

During the height of the Vietnam War, Bill Moyers was President
Lyndon Johnson's press secretary. It was his responsibility to explain
to the press and the world what was happening and why the U.S.
was doing what it was doing. He was also present as the Johnson
administration declared war on poverty, launched its Great Society
programs and signed civil rights legislation. Moyers is now one of the
most respected journalists and political analysts in the land. His is a
voice of reason and common sense, one that I have learned to trust
over the years.

He also understands the religious situation and the ideological
divide in our nation. Moyers believes that the Vietnam War and the
current military action in Iraq are among the "great blunders in our
history." So it is remarkable that he was invited to deliver a lecture on
"The Meaning of Freedom" at the United States Military Academy at
West Point last fall.

I don't know how the cadets and faculty at West Point received
the speech. That he was invited at all is a remarkable testimony to the
military's openness to dialogue, rigorous critique and dissent. I have
been consistently impressed over the years with the military academies'

openness to a diversity of opinions on topics about which one might expect the military mind to be closed.

Moyers is a political realist in the mold of Reinhold Niebuhr. He knows that we live in a world that requires us to have a strong military. Moyers understands that "the army is not a debating society."

But he also knows history, and he provided a necessary reminder of the radical principles upon which the American republic was founded. Among them are putting limits on executive power, requiring civilians to control the military and giving Congress the prerogative to declare war. The founders believed that the decision to commit the nation to war belongs to the people. Moyers pointed out that the last time the people's representatives actually declared war was 1941.

Moyers also bravely attacked the president's decision to sidestep mandates of the Geneva Convention in regard to the use of secret detentions and torture—a decision, he told the cadets, "dangerous to our honor and your welfare."

As a new year began, my attention was drawn to the coverage of the barbaric execution of Saddam Hussein and to the announcement that the number of U.S. troops killed in Iraq reached 3,000 and that the military action in Iraq is now the nation's third longest war, after Vietnam and the War for Independence. In light of those developments, it is important to hear the words of Bill Moyers, a true patriot.

FEAR NOT: A NEW KINGDOM IS HERE

January 15, 2008

What an anomaly: while many Americans were gearing up for Christmas and singing the angels' song of peace on earth, good will to all, the nation was considering the government practice of torture—or more precisely, how and why videotapes of the government's harsh interrogation practices had been destroyed.

Military experts have serious doubts about the effectiveness of torture as a means of extracting information. Under torture people will say whatever they think their tormentors want them to say. So why are we doing what seems so utterly contrary to the highest values of our nation?

About a year ago Peter Steinke wrote in these pages about the "fear factor."[1] We know about the "fight or flight" syndrome that causes eyes to widen, pupils to dilate and breathing to quicken. Steinke said there is a point at which "fear overwhelms us and actually diminishes our alertness. . . . The fearful person is barely able to focus on anything else. Tunnel vision occurs and fear takes over."

Sometimes I think that is what has happened to us as a nation. I do not mean to minimize the dangers around us. We live in a world in which some people mean to do us harm. But it seems that our fear has caused us to lay aside our principles and our reputation among the nations.

In *The Scandalous Gospel of Jesus*, Peter Gomes introduces a chapter on "the gospel of fear" with a line from Robert Frost: "There's nothing I'm afraid of like scared people." And Thomas Friedman in a *New York Times* column last September said, "9/11 has made us stupid. I honor and weep for all those murdered that day. But our reaction to 9/11, mine included, has knocked America off balance and it's time to get things right again. . . . In the wake of 9/11 we need new precautions. But we also need our old habits and sense of openness." The U.S. is doing things to prisoners, Senator John McCain said recently, that the U.S. called war crimes when they were done by the Japanese in World War II.

A passage from Isaiah 35 was read in many churches on the Third Sunday of Advent, and the words should hearten us in this new year: "Strengthen the weak hands, / And make firm the feeble knees. / Say to those of a fearful heart, / 'Be strong, do not fear! / Here is your God.'"

We have just celebrated the birth of a child who brings a new kingdom. Kindness, forgiveness, love and peace are the dynamics of God's reign. And there is nothing to fear. In that child's birth, ultimate issues have been resolved. The coming of Christ into human history, to live our life, to die our death, to defeat the power of death in his resurrection, means that the final battle has been won. It's time to stop living out of our fear—and to call the nation to do the same.

PRAYING FOR SYRIA

September 30, 2013

In the late 1930s Germany's Nazi government defied the terms of the World War I treaty and built the largest military machine in the world. Hitler invaded and occupied Poland and was beginning to persecute Jewish citizens. On the other side of the world the Japanese Empire was expanding its territorial boundaries in Southeast Asia.

In the United States, *Century* editor Charles Clayton Morrison, a "pragmatic noninterventionist," opposed American intervention or involvement in either conflict. In editorial after editorial he argued against a military buildup. Reinhold Niebuhr, a *Century* editor at large, thought that Morrison was naive and that nonintervention in the face of clear oppression and palpable evil was irresponsible. Tension between the two escalated until Niebuhr resigned and, in 1941, founded *Christianity and Crisis* to reflect what he called Christian realism. Morrison maintained his position until the Japanese attacked American forces at Pearl Harbor.

I believe that Niebuhr was right: there are times when Christians must stand against evil and oppression; there is a time to take up arms. That said, there have not been many situations that have the moral clarity and urgency of World War II. Most proposed interventions are occasions of moral complexity and incomplete or skewed information about what is happening.

Ever since the Vietnam War, I have been torn between my commitment to Christian realism and an instinct to trust the president and the government on the one hand, and the priority of peacemaking and abhorrence of violence that are essential parts of Christian faith on the other. I trusted the argument that the United States had to intervene when South Vietnam was invaded by North Vietnam. But like other Americans, I became dismayed when I realized that what we were told about the war was not true—and when death counts rose to include more than 50,000 Americans and hundreds of thousands of Vietnamese.

The same tension bedeviled me when President George W. Bush sent American troops into Iraq. I trusted Secretary of State Colin Powell and listened intently when he argued that Iraq had weapons of mass destruction—which turned out to be false.

This time the issue is a dictator's use of chemical weapons on his own people. Who wants to live in a world where that can happen without repercussion? But I'm bothered by the sense that what's happening in Syria is incredibly complex and that a missile strike by the United States might make matters worse.

My denomination's Global Ministries Division reports that Christians in Syria, our partners in mission, are adamantly opposed to American military intervention. They fear more civilian casualties, as well as the possibility that radical Islamists will respond by attacking and killing Christians.

Plans for a strike on the Syrian regime of Bashar Assad were put on hold while the United States and Russia agreed on a framework to secure and destroy Syria's chemical weapons. The two countries are negotiating on a United Nations Security Council resolution to implement the plan. The plan could easily fall apart, however, and if that happens, the United States may act militarily to punish the Assad regime.

I'm on the fence about that option. So I do what those of us on the fence ought to be doing—I pray:

> Lord of all people and all nations, your heart must break at all the reasons your children come up with to kill one another. So we humbly pray for the Syrian people caught in this deadly conflict, particularly for those who have lost dear ones. We pray for diplomats who work for peaceful resolution. We pray for the men and women of our armed forces who stand ready, on our behalf, to be in harm's way. And we pray for our president. Give him your grace. Give him wisdom to discern the right path and the courage to follow it. Amen.

CHRISTMAS TRUCE

December 18, 2014

And suddenly there was with the angel a multitude of the heavenly host, praising God and saying,

> "Glory to God in the highest heaven,
> and on earth peace among those whom he favors!"

The words strike deeply in our hearts whether recited by a child, sung by a choir, or inscribed on a greeting card. Yet peace on earth and goodwill among humans is remote. In fact, it sometimes seems that hoping for peace, expecting peace, and praying for peace is a hopeless human project.

This year marked the 100th anniversary of the beginning of the First World War. As the first mechanized war, its cost in human life was enormous and horrifying. It was to have been "the war to end all wars," but the height of tragic irony is that it was merely a prelude to a greater, more lethal war, followed by uninterrupted violence, suffering, and tragedy in the next century. Are we naive to keep talking about and hoping and praying for peace?

The Christmas truce of 1914 gave the world a glimpse of peace in a horrific time. On Christmas Eve of that year, two great armies faced each other across a front that extended along the French-Belgian border. Troops crouched in trenches cut into the soggy soil, with only candles, lanterns, and flashlights to give them light. It was a constant struggle to keep the mud walls from collapsing and the trenches from flooding.

Between the trenches was 50 to 100 yards of "no man's land." Snipers posted on each side had orders to shoot anything that moved in the opposite trench. Hand grenades were thrown, artillery shells lobbed, and occasionally soldiers charged up out of the trenches.

As Christmas approached, troops on both sides received packages from home. British troops received Princess Mary Packets—cigarettes, a greeting card from King George V, an individual plum pudding, and Cadbury chocolates. A German package included tobacco and a pipe, a profile of Crown Prince Frederick Wilhelm, and sausages and beer. The German government also sent bundles of Christmas trees to the front.

On December 24 the shooting began to slow down and then stopped altogether. No orders were given. Combatants simply stopped shooting at one another. In the early evening British troops were startled to see Christmas trees with lighted candles on the parapets of the German trench. In one spot, a German voice called out: "A gift is coming now." The British dove for cover, expecting a grenade. What came across was a boot filled with sausages. The British troops responded by sending a plum pudding and a greeting card from the king.

Then singing started: patriotic and military songs at first, followed by applause from the opposite trench. Then, breaking an eerie silence, the Germans sang "Stille Nacht, Heilige Nacht," and the British joined in, all up and down the front, on "Silent Night, Holy Night."

On Christmas Day opposing troops ventured out to extend greetings, awkward handshakes, and small gifts. In several places soccer games were played.

After a week or so the shooting resumed, and there were 6,000 deaths each day for the next 46 months.

Stanley Weintraub recounts this incident in *Silent Night: The Story of the World War I Christmas Truce*. He reflects: "The Christmas Truce has lingered strikingly in the memory . . . [it] remains a potent symbol of stubborn humanity within us."

The Christmas truce is almost too good to be true, and yet it is no more unrealistic than the angel announcing that a newborn baby is the Savior. And it is no more naive than our faith that the birth means that peace is always possible, and even close at hand.

5
Matters
of Faith

ALISDAIR MACINTYRE has taught us that a tradition is an argument about what the goods of the tradition are. If you care to weigh in on this particular family feud—you're in.

John Buchanan's tradition is that of liberal Protestantism. It has its glories—a deep desire to be as inclusive as Jesus is, a winsome face toward other faiths, a passion to see faith redound to the good of our neighborhood and world. It also has its flaws—a tendency to boil all the oddities of our faith down to a lowest common denominator that anybody can believe.

These pieces show John is a particular sort of liberal Protestant. He has a passionate belief in the particulars of the Christian faith. His essays on the high points of the Christian year resound like a drumbeat through the history of the magazine: Advent, Christmas, Lent, Easter. At each feast he unpacks the mystery with wonder, occasional skepticism, and greater surrender to the mystery. By the end, we see a sort of mystical John Buchanan—gazing on medieval portraiture of the Crucifixion in the Art Institute of Chicago, not sure about some substitutionary accounts of the atonement (who *is* sure?!), but altogether certain he's in the presence of someone worth contemplating.

I grew up among evangelicals, and one of the most

troubling patterns I notice about doctrine among mainline liberals is a tendency to identify ourselves by whatever evangelicals are not. This is, of course, just a way of being captive to evangelicals. And one thing I appreciate about John's work is he can find something to appreciate in nearly everyone—evangelicals included. Preaching should be plain, accessible, believable. He professes not only a deep belief in human fallenness—a hallmark of the *Century*'s Niebuhrian realism. He also is fascinated with holiness and seems to think God can make people holy (this Methodist heart is warmed!).

I marveled once with another luminary in John's PC(USA) church that Fourth Presbyterian still exists, going strong, doing remarkable ministry in a city like Chicago. Yes, the man said, but we used to have a dozen such vibrant churches in every great city. Conservatives say we declined because we dropped doctrine. John's pieces here show otherwise. He doesn't drop doctrine. He is mesmerized by it. And people have come to church and brought friends to watch him marvel and join in.

Liberal Protestantism, at our best, encourages serious questions. Our faith is strong enough—or maybe we should say God is strong enough—that we're not afraid of the sharpest query from the hostile-eyed teenaged confirmand or the longtime faithful octogenarian who whispers doubt like it's a shameful confession. But we don't stay in the cul-de-sac of questioning for its own sake. Questions alone wind us up in skepticism or cynicism. But faith sharpened by questions can lead to more genuine faith, or as John puts it in these pages, in "stammering praise."

IN NEED OF PRAYER

November 22, 2000

One of the theological puzzles with which I have struggled over the years is what the Puritans called "special providence"—that, is, God's miraculous intercession in human affairs in response to prayer. Every pastor knows the dilemma. We stand by the bedside of a child suffering with leukemia, holding as tightly as we can to her parents, who look to us not only for some answer to their understandable question, "Why is this happening to our child?" but also for prayers of intercession, prayers for healing.

We know the biblical mandate, "Ask and it will be given to you," and the biblical promise, "Nothing in all creation will separate us from God's love in Jesus Christ." And so we pray for healing and wholeness, covering ourselves theologically with the phrase, "if it be your will," as if the healing of a little girl could possibly not be God's will. For me the puzzle has always been complicated by the reality that there are so many children for whom no one is praying specifically.

The theological dilemma came into focus for me in a personal way recently. I was a hospital patient and people told me they were praying for me. The surgery was major but not life-threatening. My worn-out left hip was successfully replaced and I am well on the way to full recovery. My friends and colleagues told me in advance that they would pray for me and they did. Some came to the hospital and prayed. The staff of my church prayed. Members of the congregation sent me get-well cards, every single one of which announced, "We're praying for you." One of our wonderful secretaries made an appointment to see me in my office and when she arrived and sat down, told me she wanted to pray for me, which she did. The locker room attendant in the health club I frequent stunned me by looking me in the eye and saying, "God will be with you and I'll pray for you every day."

This experience doesn't solve the theological puzzle. I still can't believe that my new hip is mending more quickly because a hundred people prayed for me, while my buddy across the hall is proceeding with more difficulty because just two people are praying for him. But I do know this, in a new and profound way: strength and courage and hope and wholeness are imparted in the knowledge that others are holding you up to God in prayer. And I do know that God's healing love somehow uses the love and concern and prayers of others in the work of restoring, comforting, and creating wholeness.

And I am ready, once again, simply to be silent in the face of the mysterious goodness of God, and to resume my own pastoral ministry of praying for those whose needs are real and urgent.

RESILIENT HOPE: STAY AWAKE! BE READY!

December 19, 2001

It is generally not a good idea to refer to one's children in sermon or print, but I've concluded that when it comes to grandchildren, such rules are suspended. Rachel goes to Cardinal Bernardin School in Chicago, and as her mother was putting her to bed one night last year during Advent, she asked Rachel if she had learned any new songs at school recently. Rachel sang out of the darkness:

> Stay awake! (clap-clap)
> Be ready! (clap-clap)
> The Lord is coming soon.
> Alleluia! Alleluia! (hands waving in the air, like a wide
>   receiver after scoring a touchdown)
> The Lord is coming soon. (clap-clap)

She loves to sing it, and will sing it at the drop of a hat. So with Rachel and her sweet song, it's Advent all year long.

Advent is about hope, based on something God did in human history in Bethlehem two thousand years ago. And Advent is about hope, based on the promise that God will continue to act creatively, lovingly and redemptively in human history, and in our personal histories. Advent and the promise of Christmas come at a moment when the world desperately needs a reason to be hopeful.

Even before September 11, our culture seemed caught in a crisis of hope. Andrew Delbanco in *The Real American Dream: A Meditation in Hope* argues that "our hopes are a measure of our greatness. When our hopes shrink, we ourselves are diminished." Delbanco thinks our hopes have shrunk a lot recently, to the point where we are self-pampering.

The psychologists remind us that hopelessness is the seedbed of melancholy and destructiveness. Those of us who live in cities know how hopeless poverty breeds mindless violence. On September 11, we experienced such hopelessness nationally.

Against that backdrop, intensified this year, comes the Christian faith with its particular hopefulness. It is persistent, resilient and very old. It has lived through military catastrophes, national defeat, exile, persecution, holocaust. God's people have held tightly to hope in the darkest and most hopeless situations, and it has given them stamina, courage and life itself.

Christmas reminds us that God's hopeful love comes in ways that are not always recognizable. Nobody much recognized God's presence in Bethlehem, or later, when Jesus taught and healed and confronted and challenged. And even fewer recognized God as Jesus was betrayed, tried, convicted and crucified. We don't know how or when, but we trust that God will come into the world and into our lives with love and forgiveness and healing and reconciliation.

THE HUMAN CONDITION: WE ARE ALL COMPLICIT IN EVIL

February 27, 2002

I received a phone call once from a good friend, a member of my congregation with whom I had been carrying on an extended theological conversation for several years. She was a believer on most days, she said, and she was absolutely unafraid to doubt and hold up to scrutiny everything she thought the Christian church insisted she believe. I'll never forget that call and the conversation that followed. "I want to talk to you about something I don't like at all about our worship service," she said.

When I arrived at her apartment she had several church bulletins in her hand. As I sat down, she started to read some phrases from the Book of Common Worship: ". . . We cling to the values of a broken world. The profit and pleasure we pursue lay waste the land and pollute the seas . . . We condone evil, prejudice, warfare, and greed."

"Now really, John," she said. "I didn't do all that last week. I didn't lay waste the land and pollute the seas. I didn't have time to do all that.

I had a busy week: went shopping, volunteered at the hospital, saw a movie, went to church. Why do you make me say all those dreadful things every week?"

I did my best to tell her what the church believes and doesn't believe about sin. I told her that it doesn't believe original sin is about sex and that unbaptized babies are going to hell because they were conceived in it. I tried to tell her that sin is the human condition, that life is "not the way it's supposed to be," to cite the title of Cornelius Plantinga's solid book. I tried to tell her about Reinhold Niebuhr's observation that the doctrine of original sin is the one empirically verifiable doctrine of Christian faith and that all you have to do to know about sin and its effects is to read the newspaper. I told her that even though she and I did not personally "lay waste the earth and pollute the seas," we did participate in political and economic structures that are plenty guilty of both. It was a hard sell, and I'm not sure she bought it or that afterward she used the public confession in worship any more comfortably.

I thought about that conversation as I read the articles on Rwanda and South Africa in this issue. They made me very uncomfortable. They also made me appreciate that moment in public worship where we admit our complicity, even though unintended, in unspeakable evil. It makes me grateful for the Lenten journey that moves inexorably toward the cross and for the mystery of a love big enough to overcome even our sin.

STAMMERING PRAISE: IN GOOD AND NOT-SO-GOOD TIMES

November 20, 2002

When I was a youngster my parents always took me to community Thanksgiving services. I was an unwilling and unhappy participant. I didn't much like them: there weren't many people there, I didn't know most of those who were, and I surely didn't care for the preaching. "Why do we have to attend these things every year?" My mother answered, "Because of the hymns. They're the best in the book."

She was right, of course. Karl Barth once said that the basic human response to God is not fear and trembling, not guilt and dread, but thanksgiving. "What else can we say to what God gives us but to stammer praise?" Barth asked. And what better way to stammer than with "Come Ye Thankful People Come," or "We Gather Together to Ask the Lord's Blessing" or "Now Thank We All Our God, with Heart and Hand and Voices," which the late Robert McAfee Brown once said is the best all-purpose hymn, suitable for every important occasion—birth, baptism, wedding, ordination or funeral.

Currier and Ives–type portrayals have romanticized that first Thanksgiving, which was actually pretty harrowing. Half of those hearty souls who left Plymouth and sailed to Holland and then crossed the Atlantic to New England died after one year in the new world. All but three families had dug graves in the rocky soil of New England to bury a husband, wife or child. They had brought plants and seeds with them on the Mayflower, along with provisions for the first winter. The barley they planted did very poorly. The peas failed altogether. Starvation was a real possibility.

They were, of course, people of the Bible. They knew about ancient Israel's harvest festival, how Israel, at the end of a successful harvest, thanked God for the bounty of creation—and also for delivering them from their captivity, giving them their freedom as a people.

The Pilgrim fathers and mothers read their own story in light of Israel's story. God is thanked for the harvest, but also for something more, something not actually dependent on a successful harvest: namely, God's presence and grace and love. The Pilgrims thanked God for enough corn to survive the winter, but they were also thanking God for the guiding presence they had experienced, the strong hand they had felt leading them, and the love that had sustained them. They understood that God is to be thanked and praised in good times and not-so-good times.

One of the saints of our generation, Abraham Joshua Heschel, suffered a heart attack from which he never fully recovered. A friend who visited him in the hospital found him weak and barely able to talk. "Sam," he whispered, "when I regained consciousness, my first feeling was not despair and anger. I felt only gratitude to God for my life, for every moment I have lived. . . . I have seen so many miracles."

WHY, GOD? THE BIGGEST AND MOST
PROFOUND QUESTIONS OF ALL

January 25, 2005

Perhaps it was John Wesley who observed that a preacher has only a few things to say, only a few sermons to preach, and that the task of preaching is a matter of addressing in newly creative and energetic ways the few essential themes. After four decades of preaching, I'm ready to agree. The few sermons we all have are related to the basic questions people ask—about guilt and grace, forgiveness and restoration, life and death, the reality of evil and suffering and the goodness of God.

The lectionary Psalm for the second Sunday in January was Psalm 29: "The voice of the Lord is over the water." Those words powerfully intersected with the news of the horrific deaths and suffering caused by the tsunami in South Asia. They present us clearly with the questions that are on the minds of so many: Why did God do this or allow this to happen? Where was God? What is God? Such questions lurk also in calmer times, beneath the surface of comfortable lives.

Among the most worn and underlined books in my library are the ones that offer some help in understanding, framing and responding to these questions. They include:

A Cry of Absence: Reflections for the Winter of the Heart, by Martin E. Marty (Harper & Row, 1983). This is a beautiful book, written after the death of the author's first wife, which employs the Psalter to explore the silence and absence of God in the heart broken by loss. Marty's daughter-in-law Susan contributed spare, elegant sketches for each chapter.

Lament for a Son, by Nicholas Wolterstorff (Eerdmans, 1987). A Yale philosopher writes poetically and authentically about the death of his 25-year-old son. His brief diary entries speak to my mind and heart: "To the most agonized question I have ever asked I do not know the answer. I do not know why God would watch him fall."

Why, God? by Burton Z. Cooper (John Knox, 1988). The author, a teacher of theology at Louisville Seminary, writes following the death of a daughter. He brings to the conversation C. S. Lewis, Albert Camus, Fyodor Dostoevsky, Karl Barth and Dietrich Bonhoeffer.

The Cross in Our Context: Jesus and the Suffering World, by Douglas John Hall (Fortress, 2003). Hall has been my mentor from afar ever since I read *Lighten Our Darkness* in 1979. His three-volume *Theology in a North American Context* has kept me busy for years. And the question of God's love and the reality of human suffering has been at the center of Hall's quest. In his most recent book Hall returns to his concern that Western Christendom eagerly adopted the Theology of Glory and ignored the Theology of the Cross. He is most helpful in his careful explication of God's self-limited power for the sake of God's love—which is the only treatment of God and suffering that is sensible and healing for me.

I am grateful for all those who have struggled so honestly and faithfully with the biggest and most profound questions of all.

GIFT WRAPPED: GOD'S PLAN TO CALL LOVE OUT OF US

December 12, 2006

My neighborhood offers Christmas shoppers lots of help: the counters are full, and the windows have been elegantly displaying gift suggestions since mid-October. I am led to ponder the original gift that generated this phenomenon of Christmas—a small, quiet, intimate gift of love in the birth of a child. What this is about, I remind myself, is God and God's love and God's plan to call love out of us.

The Greeks taught that God is perfect. By that they meant that God is complete, that God has no needs, no hopes, no aspirations. God doesn't need anything. God's perfection, the Greeks thought, meant that God is isolated, unchanging, unfeeling. The Greek word for it is *apatheia*. If God had feelings, became angry or happy, hated or loved, God would be as vulnerable as any human being—a preposterous idea, they thought.

Then came a new idea—that God loves, that God is love, love with all the risk and vulnerability and heartbreak that go along with love. Douglas John Hall says that the basic Christian assertion is the opposite of the Greek idea: "God is God only in relationship," Hall wrote. God cares so deeply, loves so passionately, that it hurts.

Twenty centuries ago a man by the name of John wrote to a beleaguered church in Asia Minor: "Beloved, let us love one another, because love is from God. . . . God is love and those who abide in love abide in God, and God abides in them."

That's the bottom line. God is love. Those who love live in God and God lives in them. The highest and best of our humanity occurs when we love one another, when we care for and respect one another. We are put here to love, Sister Joan Chittister says, not for the sake of the other alone, but for our sake as well.

To be able to love, to have love planted in your heart, to have love called out of you, is to be alive. The perfect gift is a gift that awakens your own love, that draws love out of you—perhaps against your will or better judgment, your normally cautious reserve that warns you to be careful, not to care too much, not to risk being hurt, not to be extravagant.

That is what Christmas is: God coming to the world in love—humble, vulnerable, weak love; God coming in the birth of a child; God coming to refashion us into the men and women we are intended to be. "God is love, and those who abide in love abide in God, and God abides in them."

CITY SCENE: EVERYDAY KINDNESS

May 15, 2007

Sometimes life in a big city can feel impersonal, almost inhuman. On the streets the taxis vie for pole position at the stoplights and cut one another off to get to a fare. On the sidewalks people beg for money, holding signs that say things like "Homeless. Hungry. Help."

But sometimes the city feels so grace-filled it almost makes me weep. I often ride the bus from the church where I work on North Michigan Avenue in Chicago to the offices of the *Century* on South Michigan. The bus takes twice as long as a cab, but it costs much less and almost always yields something interesting.

The other day I got on the No. 151 bus and started to read. At the next stop I watched as an elderly white woman boarded the bus and wasn't sure about how to use her transit card. She inserted it upside down, then backward. While the other passengers became increasingly distressed by the delay, the driver, a very pleasant African-American woman, patiently explained how to use the card. "Here, honey, let me do it for you," she said, leaning out of her seat, one hand on the wheel. The woman finally walked toward a seat but then turned back. "Are you sure it took only one fare from my card?" she asked the driver. "I heard it beep twice." "Yes, I'm sure," the driver answered. "But I heard it beep twice: it took two fares." "No, honey: it only took one fare. It always beeps twice." "How do you know?" the woman demanded. "Here, let me show you. Come on up here and look at the indicator. There it is, your one fare." By this time the stoplight had cycled from red to green twice. Finally we were under way.

At the stop after that a man in a motorized chair pulled the cord. He was frail, and one could see the tubes from the oxygen tank that was helping him breathe. "I'm on my way to the V.A. hospital and I'm going to need some help," he announced. Again the driver responded graciously. She helped him negotiate his motorized chair to the door, told him how to position the chair for the mechanical lift, asked him to adjust the position an inch or two, and then activated the lift. The process took a long time. You could sense the tension and impatience of the people on the bus. The stoplight cycled a few more times and motorists honked. The driver, unfazed, remained infinitely patient. She was a note of grace on that busy urban thoroughfare. As I got off the bus, I thanked her for her kindness. "Just doing my job," she said. "You have a blessed day now, honey."

GOOD NEWS IN BRIEF

August 31, 2012

Art and Helen Romig were memorable people in my life. Art's parents were Presbyterian missionaries; he grew up in China at a time when the Presbyterians alone had 500 missionary workers in China. He studied at the College of Wooster in Ohio, then attended Princeton Seminary. Art courted Helen, a social worker in New York City, and they married and returned to China as missionaries. Helen and the children were evacuated to the U.S. during the Japanese occupation; Art was held in a prison camp for several years. After the war the Romigs returned to China but were sent home again, this time by the new communist government.

Art continued his ministry as a pastor and presbytery executive before "retiring" to central Ohio, where I met him. He joined the staff of the congregation I was serving, and we worked together until he retired again, this time to Santa Fe, New Mexico.

Helen, an accomplished artist, had a collection of ancient Chinese gravestone rubbings that were of interest to Chicago's Field Museum. They were invited to visit the museum, and my wife and I hosted the Romigs during their stay. One night we ate dinner at a Chinese restaurant. Art ordered for us in Chinese, of course, and before we knew it he was engaged in a lively, animated exchange with our waiter. The young man hurried off, and Art said, "Wait till you see this!"

Suddenly the wait and kitchen staff had gathered around our table and were engaged in an enthusiastic and increasingly chaotic discussion. Art explained to us that the entire staff, all students at the University of Illinois at Chicago, were from the village in western China where Art and Helen had lived and served years before. Art was inquiring about people he'd known there, some of whom he'd baptized. It was an unforgettable reminder of the reach of the global church.

Whenever I preached a sermon that was a little dense, with one too many references to illuminate an obscure point, Art would gently explain that one of the skills mission workers had to learn was to articulate the gospel simply. The proclamation of the gospel, Art said, should never be intellectually anemic but simple and direct enough that anyone could understand it.

In this issue we asked a few of our favorite authors to proclaim "The gospel in seven words" (or fewer). The pithy responses remind me of Art's wise advice. In our culture, the basic Christian vocabulary is increasingly esoteric to many. It's a useful exercise to say it simply, in a way anyone can understand.

THE ULTIMATE MYSTERY

March 21, 2014

Russia's recent incursion into Crimea has brought back memories of the cold war. George F. Kennan, a scholar, historian, and State Department adviser, is known as the father of America's "containment policy," which was based on his conviction that the Soviet Union was expansionistic and that world peace depended on the United States and its allies containing Soviet territorial ambitions.

Kennan later became an eloquent critic of a U.S. foreign policy that favored dialogue with the Soviets. In perspective, some of his ideas and suggestions have been helpful, some not. I loved his 1993 book, *Around the Cragged Hill: A Personal and Political Philosophy.*

In a recent issue of the *New York Times* (February 23), journalist Fareed Zakaria reviewed *The Kennan Diaries*, a collection of Kennan's essays, letters, and meanderings.[1] I was surprised when Zakaria said: "Kennan's views were rooted in history, philosophy, and—somewhat surprising to me—faith." On Good Friday, 1980, Kennan wrote in his diary:

> Most human events yield to the erosion of time. The greatest, most amazing exception to this generalization . . . A man, a Jew, some sort of dissident religious prophet, was crucified. . . . In the teachings of this man were two things: first, the principle of charity of love . . . secondly, the possibility of redemption in the face of self-knowledge and penitence. . . . The combination of these two things . . . shaped and disciplined the minds and values of many generations—placed, in short, its creative stamp on one of the greatest flowerings of the human spirit.

This season I've adopted a new discipline—a Lenten pilgrimage, albeit a brief one. I walk across the street from the *Century* office to the Art Institute of Chicago, climb the stairs to the second floor, and spend an hour or so in the Middle Ages and Renaissance galleries. Many of the paintings are of the crucifixion. In every age, including our own, this event has compelled artists and musicians with its raw human drama as well as its deeper meanings: innocent suffering, redemption, forgiveness, and hope. The result is some of the most sublime art and music ever created.

The crucifixion has challenged Christianity's best thinkers, who created various atonement theologies. I've been thinking about this unlikely claim all my life: that this brutal event has ultimate transcendent significance, that God is in it. I have found myself moving away from the notion that God intended, planned, and choreographed the crucifixion and away from the related idea that Jesus had to die a sacrificial lamb to satisfy an offended and angry deity.

My thinking has been shaped by years of listening to and praying with people who are suffering and by my own experience. I believe that parenting tells us much about God. As parents we give our children the freedom to risk tragedy and, when they suffer, we do everything we can to take on that suffering ourselves. Other relationships teach us the same truths. As C. S. Lewis said, to love anyone is to open oneself to heartbreak.

The most radical thing anyone ever said about the ultimate mystery is this: God loves us so much as to be with us in our suffering, to take into God's own self our most profound experience, to be at one with us.

FAITH CONFIRMED

June 4, 2014

When we were expecting our first grandchild, a friend put his arm around my shoulder and solemnly said, "John, you are about to experience the only truly free lunch." He was right.

From the vantage point of years, we grandparents understand that what we thought were crises were not so serious after all and that whether or not the children ate their Brussels sprouts had nothing to do with the kind of people they turned out to be. Nor am I the first to observe that grandchildren grow quickly. One day you're reading a toddler a story and the next thing you know she's looking you in the eye and asking if you remember the Vietnam War.

It was with this sense of time passing that our family gathered recently for the confirmation of our granddaughter Eleanor. At the beginning of her confirmation class, her father had told me that Eleanor wasn't certain that she wanted to join the church; in fact, she wasn't certain that she believed in God. I assured him that her concerns were typical and not inappropriate. After eight months of weekly classes, retreats, and mission trips, however, Eleanor told me that she loved her confirmation class experience and had decided to declare her faith and become a member of the congregation.

I thought about my own confirmation experience, when eight of us seventh graders were supposed to memorize the answers to 107 catechetical questions. Some of them are doozies. Question 4: "What is God?" Answer: "God is Spirit, infinite, eternal, and unchangeable, in his being, wisdom, power, holiness, justice, goodness, and truth." The churchmen who drafted the Westminster Confession and the Larger and Shorter Catechisms were confident that the reality of God could be nailed down in language. I'm not certain what the experience did for me, but I've always been glad to remember the answer to the first question: "Man's chief end is to glorify God and to enjoy him forever."

After Eleanor's confirmation I went home and picked up James Fowler's *Becoming Adult, Becoming Christian.* Fowler says adult faith happens as a result of developing, among other things, "a deep habitus, a pervasive orientation to the divine initiative and the universality in love."

In Eleanor's class, the pastor asked each of the 27 members to write a statement of faith (something that would never have occurred in my day).

Eleanor wrote: "Everyone is a child of God—even if you don't believe in God, you still are. I believe you can see God in anyone. I believe Jesus was God's son. Through the friends I have made and the discussion in my circle group, I have never seen God more clearly. I have been going to church all my life, but I never thought about God in a deep way. . . . This year I loved going to church and the sense of community I feel. The most significant thing I learned this year is to love my neighbor just as Jesus taught us."

Eleanor concluded by saying she wanted to be a part of the wonderful things the church does.

Reciting answers to catechetical questions and memorizing scripture are good things to do. But as I read Eleanor's statement of faith and watched her kneel in front of the congregation and become part of the body of Christ, I felt hope for the church and my heart was full of gratitude.

6
Popular
Culture

THE CHURCH HAS long noticed, and had to account for, intimations of the gospel far outside our walls. Origen compared truth outside the church to the Egyptians' treasure, which Israel plunders to take and beautify their future temple. Augustine shrugged and figured any truth is God's truth. Karl Barth talked of secular parables—witnesses that God will not hesitate to raise up if the church won't praise properly.

More recently, with the collapse of Christendom, we've had to navigate what to do when a hostile media makes a hash of what we believe. Some of pop culture raises up things that look a lot like Jesus. Other elements of it take aim at faith and hit the straw man it has built.

John spots the outlines of Jesus in quite vulgar media (Oprah and Osteen) and in quite serious music (Rostropovich and Brubek). And of course John could not fail at least once or twice a summer to sermonize on the virtues of his Chicago Cubs, who managed to make a virtue out of losing (back then anyway). What will John do if the Cubs ever actually win a World Series? Walter Brueggemann, a longtime friend of the magazine and fan of the Cubs' nemesis downriver, the St. Louis Cardinals, says he has a verse for the Cubs from Jeremiah: "Summer is over, and we are not saved" (Jer. 8:20).

Perhaps what makes John such a compelling preacher,

writer, and church leader is that he's never lost a capacity for wonder. He's simply amazed at life. He's paying attention. And he wants others to see what he's looking at. I'll never get out of my mind the image of Rostropovich, the great cellist, playing as the Berlin Wall is coming down. Nor the image of him kissing and hugging fellow musicians as he exits the stage, having first, of course, kissed his beloved cello. I'll not forget the image of Brubek hollering out that John is "my pastor" when he sees him, nor the image of young John cheering on Larry Doby in the 1948 World Series.

You can discern a hint of John rebuking us mainline academics here. He agrees fully that Oprah is superficial. Osteen is horrifying. And Peale is, as some wag once put it, appalling (while St. Paul is appealing). And yet, with all our proud sophistication, have we missed something these popularizers are offering? And shouldn't we give thanks that God is using them to make folks' lives just a little bit better? If we don't like it, let's knock ourselves out and produce something better that folks might actually want to watch or read. With popular culture, the criticism doesn't just go one way.

The Westminster Shorter Catechism famously proclaims that our chief end as human beings is to "glorify God and enjoy God forever." And so it is on our screens, in the movie theater, the baseball stadium, the music hall, the sanctuary, the world.

CAN YOU GIVE YOUR WITNESS?

September 25, 2002

I must confess I had never heard of Oprah Winfrey before she appeared in the role of Sofia in the 1985 film version of Alice Walker's novel *The Color Purple*. It was a difficult and demanding part, and I remember being impressed with the power of her portrayal. Roger Ebert called Oprah's Sofia an "indomitable force of nature." I also recall learning that Oprah's own experience had prepared her, in some way, for the role.

Since that time, Oprah has become one of the most influential people in America. Her book club successfully encouraged people to read serious books. She lives in the neighborhood where the church I serve is located, and people around here compare notes on occasional Oprah sightings. I actually met her once when she very graciously attended a reception for her friend Maya Angelou, who was speaking at our church's Arts Festival.

If, like me, you have regarded Oprah as simply another day-time talk show host, Marcia Z. Nelson's article ("Oprah on a Mission") may change your mind. And you might find that Nelson's list of ten reasons why Oprah is compelling offers useful material for a clergy job description.

I am also intrigued by Nelson's suggestion that Oprah's show is "not just talk, but talk that's been refined in life's fires—talk as testimony." It reminds me of something I learned and experienced listening to James Forbes lead a preaching workshop a long time ago. Forbes, now pastor at Riverside Church in New York, began by having a little fun with us mainline-denomination types. He said some sermons have about as much passion as a corporate CEO's report to the stockholders. And then he started to talk about "preaching as testimony." "How long has it been since you gave your testimony?" he asked. We all shifted uneasily in our seats, sensing where he was going.

"Let's have testimony time," he said." Right here, right now, no notes, no pulpit to hide behind. Just stand up and give your testimony. Tell us what the Spirit has been doing in your life recently."

What followed wasn't, as they say, very pretty. We did it, but we were not in familiar territory. After we had each managed to say something about what the Spirit was doing in our lives, Forbes remarked, "You don't have to do that from the pulpit. But if you don't believe the gospel and have some experience of its truth, you have no right to expect your people to." I've never forgotten that lesson about the power of testimony.

GOOD INNINGS: JACKIE ROBINSON'S SUCCESSOR

July 26, 2003

It's high summer, and those of us who measure time by the mystical rhythms of baseball are deeply immersed in the game. We have been talking lately about the Sammy Sosa affair. The Chicago Cubs slugger embarrassed himself by getting caught—on television no less—using a "corked" bat. He was banished for seven games, during which the baseball faithful argued about the nature of the infraction: Did he know the bat was corked? Had he been using corked bats consistently? Had the cork helped him hit 70 home runs in one season? For what it's worth, I think that he knew, and that the cork didn't help him at all.

The feat of hitting a baseball thrown by a pitcher at speeds approaching 100 miles an hour, some of which are curve balls which appear to be coming toward your head and then swoop across the plate at the last moment, is something of a miracle. To hit consistently, and to hit the ball out of the park consistently, is an amazing feat. Sosa does just that.

A few days after returning from his suspension, he hit a prodigious home run that traveled 520 feet and landed in the street outside Wrigley Field. The phone rang and it was Johnny, my six-year-old grandson, who was watching the game on television. "Did you see it, Granddaddy? Did you see Sammy hit it?" We talked and oohed and aahed and shared a moment of wonder and awe.

I was reminded of my first true baseball love, back when I was just a few years older than Johnny: the 1948 Cleveland Indians. I was a Pirates fan, but somehow my eye was caught by the Indians. The team had the great pitcher Bob Feller, player-manager Lou Boudreau, and a graceful center fielder by the name of Larry Doby. Doby was an African-American, the first to play in the American League. Jackie Robinson was the first in either league, introduced by the Brooklyn Dodgers in 1947. Doby followed later that season. My father took me to Pittsburgh to see Robinson when the Dodgers visited the Pirates that summer. My problem with Robinson was that he was a Dodger and the Dodgers routinely beat my Pirates.

The Indians won the World Series in 1948 and I was in heaven. I have followed Larry Doby over the years: his induction into the Hall of Fame and his front-office work for the Indians. He died a few days ago, a quiet, graceful man who endured this country's worst racism and rose above it, in the process helping to change a sport and a culture. Fay Vincent, a former commissioner of Major League Baseball, commented that Doby showed a total lack of bitterness or resentment about the racism he encountered. Doby himself said, "I was never bitter because I believed in the man upstairs. I continue to do my best. If I was bitter I'd only be hurting me." Vincent wrote in the *New York Times* on Doby's death: "In an age when we struggle to identify true heroes, Larry Doby is one of mine." Mine too.

LOW TECH: MEMBERSHIP LISTS IN A SHOE BOX

August 23, 2003

I am not a high-tech person. That's partly due to age, partly to disposition. The very mention of my technological skills sets my colleagues and family to snickering. I never thought I'd be an anachronism and I'm not particularly proud of it. But I do find myself resisting some of the places the new technology wants to take me. So I appreciate David Wood's interview with Albert Borgmann ("Prime Time"), who has been thinking about how technology shapes a culture and a way of life. He urges us to put bounds on our use of technology.

That makes me think, of course, about the importance of turning off the television. And it makes me think about the omnipresence of cell phones. I'm not the only preacher whose homiletical momentum has been brought to a halt by a ringing cell phone. The best, or worst, incident happened recently during a wedding rehearsal. As we were practicing the vows, the groom's phone rang. He extracted it from his coat pocket, answered and handed it to the bride. "It's for you," he said.

I know the blessing and the curse. The church's software system sometimes sends "please pay your pledge" notices to church members who died several years ago. (My colleagues roll their eyes when I remind them that things like that didn't happen when we kept the membership lists on 3 x 5 cards in a shoe box.) Sometimes e-mail capability encourages people to say more than they should to each other.

On the other hand, the e-mail daily devotions that arrive on members' computer screens extend and deepen the community of faith. The church can communicate with members, boards and committees with an ease and efficiency that are amazing and certainly enhance a sense of community. Several of our church members were among the first troops to go to Iraq, and we were able to communicate with them and extend pastoral care in a new and wonderful way.

As Borgmann suggests, it's important to set limits. I plan to hold tightly to what Borgmann calls "focal" activities that define your life at its best and most authentic—like reading, eating and talking with the people you love, walking in the early morning, writing a letter, reading a book. And I don't really want to go back to the shoebox and the 3 x 5 cards.

TAKEN UP: BEING PREPARED

April 20, 2004

In discussing two books on the new apocalypticism, Jason Byassee ("En-raptured") confesses that he failed as a pastor to know what his people were reading and thinking about the topic. I know what he means. I don't read this stuff either. But a lot of people *are* reading it. Sales estimates for the Left Behind series range from 40 million to 60 million. Whatever the exact figure, authors Tim LaHaye and Jerry Jenkins are surpassing John Grisham in the category of popular novelists. The publisher, Tyndale House, knows a good thing when it sees it: it will spend $2 million marketing the 12th and final volume, *Glorious Appearing*. Wal-Mart is giving away free copies of the first chapter as a come-on.

Joseph Hough, president of Union Theological Seminary in New York, told the *New York Times* that the Left Behind series and the apocalyptic theology it is based on represent a "serious distortion of scripture."[1] It is certainly bloody. When Jesus returns to battle the Antichrist's armies it will be a ghastly massacre. "Tens of thousands of foot soldiers writhing . . . Their innards and entrails gushed to the desert floor."

My attitude has been elitist, I confess. I don't take this stuff seriously. When I see a bumper sticker that announces: "Warning: In case of rapture this vehicle will be unmanned," I chuckle, remembering that a friend once said she thought the reference to "rapture" in the bumper sticker referred to something sexual happening in the front seat. And I remember that my grandmother, who late in life picked up theology from radio evangelists, believed that the Final Tribulation had begun in her lifetime. Grandma, as I recall, for a while regarded FDR as the Antichrist. Then it was Hitler. Next it was Stalin.

What are pastors to do in a religious climate in which millions of people are buying, reading, enjoying and maybe even believing that history is headed toward an enormous bloodbath? We should take seriously the fact that people do ask: What will the end be? Is there some final purpose at work in human history?

For another thing, we should be prepared with biblical alternatives such as Jeremiah 31—in which the prophet looks ahead and sees a time of reunion, when God's people will return home with tears of consolation, young women will dance, young and old men will be merry, and mourning will be transformed into joy. Or St. Paul, asking the eschatological questions in light of his experience of Christ's Lordship: "a plan for the fullness of time, to gather up all things in him, things in heaven and on earth" (Eph. 1:10).

Two things I am going to do: put Byassee's article into my Eschatology/Apocalyptic file (I know they're different categories!) and put Amy Frykholm's and Barbara Rossing's books on the top of my stack for summer reading.

UP FOR REVIEW: VENTURES INTO POPULAR CULTURE

June 1, 2004

Like many ministers, I used the popularity of Mel Gibson's film *The Passion of the Christ* to focus attention in the church on what we believe about Jesus Christ. But I declined to tell people whether or not they should buy a ticket to see the film.

At the end of my series of sermons related to it, a friend pushed back gently by suggesting that I was wrong to say that the world is divided between people who love *The Passion* and those who hate it. "There's a third group," she said. "We may be bigger than the other two, and we're feeling a little marginalized. We're the ones who aren't going to see the movie, who won't go to any violent movies because we think violence in the media contributes to the violence all around us. We don't care about the movie, and we think you are paying entirely too much attention to it." She went on: "There are two kinds of people: those who think there are two kinds of people and those who know there are many kinds."

Chastened by this critique and feeling a little defensive, I set to thinking again about how we relate popular culture to our faith, and how we use it in our preaching and writing, our thinking and theologizing. What's the appropriate level of engagement with the culture around us? At the risk of dichotomizing once more, I'd say there are two risks. The first is to turn our backs on the world, retreating to our sanctuaries and studies. This is, of course, an old and persistent temptation. The other risk is that we will pay too much attention to popular culture and, with the aim of being relevant and timely, simply mirror the culture's idolatries and preoccupations.

It is not easy to find the balance, but finding it is important. At this magazine, we talk a lot about finding that balance. We have some reservations about the culture and the agenda it sets, and about many movies and books that occupy center stage. But we also want to be timely and helpful. So we do venture into the arena of popular culture with articles on Oprah Winfrey, *The Simpsons* and *The Da Vinci Code*—not to mention *The Passion* (our articles on that film generated more mail than did any other topic in years).

Here is another venture into popular culture: If you are wondering what to read this summer, I recommend Stuart Dybek's *The Coast of Chicago*, a collection of short stories about growing up on Chicago's gritty streets. I know I'm enjoying a book when I slow down in order to savor each page. The book is this year's choice for the "One Book—One Chicago" program, selected by the mayor's office and the Public Library Board to encourage citywide reading.

In one of the stories, two irreverent, tough young men stand outside the prison complex on California Avenue yelling to their friend Pancho, who is somewhere inside. They know he's going to disappear into that vast, demonic system, and they remember how Pancho used to drag them along to visit seven parish churches on Good Friday because it was his favorite holiday. You'll like this book.

POSITIVE INFLUENCE: THE GOSPEL OF REWARD FILLS A MAINLINE VACUUM

July 26, 2005

The article in the previous issue on megachurch pastor Joel Osteen set me to thinking about the members of my congregation who are watching Osteen on television and reading his books.[2] The situation reminds me of the lament of the Reverend John Ames (in Marilynne Robinson's novel *Gilead*): 40 years of careful, literate, theologically sound preaching could be undone in a 20-minute sermon by a radio preacher.

In his review of Osteen's "gospel of reward," Jason Byassee noted that Osteen is something of an "easy target" for theological critique. During my seminary years a similar target was Norman Vincent Peale. Peale was a friend of prominent business and industry leaders and U.S. presidents. His books were hugely successful. Just about everybody read *The Power of Positive Thinking*. But professors had a field day with him, pointing out that his books were light, his sermons not biblical, his theology shallow to nonexistent, his positive thinking the opposite of the realistic assessment of the human condition as described by Augustine and Calvin, not to mention Nietzsche, Freud and Marx.

I shared this view until I met John Boyle. He came to Chicago to direct a counseling center at the church I serve, one of the first of its kind and a critically important resource in our community. Peale had been his pastor. Peale baptized Boyle when he was 12 and began to show an interest in his spiritual development. When it came time for college, Peale helped him gain admittance to Bucknell. When World War II interrupted Boyle's college career Peale continued to follow him by mail through infantry battles in France and Germany and the liberation of Dachau. After the war, friendship with Peale led Boyle to theological seminary, a doctorate in psychology and a very distinguished ministry.

Of course, Peale's books *were* light. But they also were the way thousands upon thousands of people first considered the possibility that they mattered to God, that whatever suffering or unhappiness they might be experiencing was not caused by God, that God's will for them was a full and joyful life. We mainliners have always been a little reticent about saying those kinds of things. And so people turn to the Peales and Osteens like thirsty people to water.

The other day I heard from a young parishioner, recently married, who had just received devastating news from her doctor. She was asking me to pray for her. She added: "I've been reading a book by Joel Osteen, *Your Best Life Now*. I have slowly begun to realize that I am in God's favor."

Any theology that promises success as a reward for faithfulness and fervent prayer is misleading at best, and it deserves a forceful critique. At the same time I've learned not to dismiss ministries, however different from mine, that can lead people to their vocation or to a new sense of God's love.

BRAVO! EXTRAVAGANT DISPLAYS OF LOVE

July 10, 2007

High on the list of people I have most admired is Mstislav Rostropovich, the great Russian cellist who died in April. I admired him first for his courage. In 1970 Rostropovich expressed his support for artistic freedom and human rights in a letter to Pravda, the state-run newspaper of the Soviet Union. In response, the Soviets stripped him and his wife of Soviet citizenship.

I also admired his passion for life, his exuberance and his propensity to show great love. I heard him play a Dvorak cello concerto, one of his favorites, in Chicago, and at the end of the performance, as the audience sat in silence, mesmerized, Rostropovich did an extraordinary thing: he stood up and kissed his cello. The audience erupted. Then he hugged and kissed a surprised Daniel Barenboim, the conductor. Then he hugged and kissed the entire cello section before moving on to the violins. He hugged and kissed most of the members of the orchestra.

Years later, I had the honor of meeting him at a dinner party. He insisted on sitting beside a high school cellist—my granddaughter. So I ended up sitting on the other side of him. He spent most of the evening in conversation with my granddaughter. When he finally turned to me, I told him I had been moved by a video showing him playing Bach in front of the Berlin Wall in 1989, as the wall was being torn down and communism was breaking apart throughout Eastern Europe. He told me the whole story: how, when he and his wife heard news of the wall coming down and knew that their own nation would soon be free, they had to do something. He flew to Berlin with his cello and took a cab to the wall, and then realized that he hadn't thought about a chair to sit on. He knocked on the door of the first house he came to, introduced himself and asked if he could borrow a chair.

He invited me to call him by the affectionate name, "Slava," that his friends used. At the end of our extraordinary evening, he called for a toast, Russian style. We toasted Russia and the United States; we toasted freedom, J. S. Bach, the Dallas Symphony Orchestra and my granddaughter. Then he hugged and kissed all of us.

His love for music, for freedom and for people was contagious. Many of us who have been taught to curtail emotional displays could learn a thing or two about wholeness and about love truly expressed from this extraordinary human being. I thought about him during a week when I pondered again the story in Luke 7 about a nameless woman, "a sinner," who was also passionate and extravagant in showing love.

BEAUTIFUL GAMES: THE WORLD CUP

August 3, 2010

The rest of the world calls it "the beautiful game," and for a month of World Cup soccer competition Americans get to see it on TV—the moments of explosive action and the constant flow of movement from one end of the field to the other, with hardly any commercial interruptions. More Americans (19.4 million) recently watched Ghana eliminate the U.S. in the World Cup than, on average, watched a World Series game last year.

Soccer generates passionate loyalties that sometimes erupt into violence. National teams become symbols of national identity. Americans were sorry to see their team eliminated, but the loss did not evoke the intense grief felt by the people of many other nations when their teams suffered defeat.

Baseball is another beautiful game that inspires deep passions. I fell in love with baseball listening to radio broadcasts of the Pittsburgh Pirates while sitting with my father on our front porch. Rosie Rosewell was the announcer and Bob Prince provided the color commentary. When Pirate slugger Ralph Kiner hit a home run, Rosewell would blow a whistle and say, "Open the window, Aunt Minnie, here she comes!"

This year the Chicago Cubs, my hometown team, looked sound, even promising, at the beginning of the season. Management had assembled the third-highest player payroll in the major leagues. But bad things seem to happen to the Cubs. This year, highly paid pitchers have not performed well. The ace of the staff was sent off to address anger-management issues. Sluggers have not been slugging and Gold Glove infielders have been committing errors. Base runners have been getting picked off.

After each game the manager faces the cameras and confesses that he's tried everything he can think of. The team seems afflicted with what Kierkegaard calls a sickness unto death. Redemption is not in sight.

My dad bought me an official baseball score book when I was young and taught me how to score the game. As a boy I did it for virtually every game. I still mark the scorecard when I go to watch the Cubs. It not only helps you focus on what's happening, it provides historical context—which, as biblical scholars know, means everything. It's important to know that the hitter at the plate has struck out twice already.

On a delightful day this summer I was in my seat at the Cubs game, with my ten-year-old granddaughter beside me. She showed interest in my written record of what was happening on the field, and soon she was holding the scorecard and marking down DP: 6-4-3 for a double play, and a K for a strikeout, and a backward K for a called third strike.

The Cubs lost badly that day, but it was still a beautiful game. And the row of scorecards on my shelf, next to the biblical commentaries, bear silent witness to biblical virtues: patience, endurance, steadfastness, hope—and love.

REMEMBERING BRUBECK

January 7, 2013

When jazz legend Dave Brubeck died on December 5, his profound impact on the world of jazz was noted by front-page announcements of his death in newspapers all over the world. Along with millions of others, I was a devoted Dave Brubeck fan ever since I first heard his music in the 1950s.

Brubeck changed jazz by producing his "cool" sound in collaboration with alto saxophonist Paul Desmond, who played counterpoint to Brubeck's piano. Their innovative use of unusual rhythms captured the imagination of a generation of college students in the '50s and '60s. His 33 rpm record *Time Out* became the first jazz album to sell more than a million copies. After a tour of India and the Middle East, Brubeck began to experiment with rhythmic structures. His signature piece comes from his collaboration with Desmond, "Take Five," perhaps the most popular jazz single ever. He also composed a lively Christmas piece, "God's Love Made Visible," in 5/4 time.

Brubeck's father was an avowed atheist, while his mother, a Christian Scientist, directed the choir at a Presbyterian church. Brubeck's first job was playing the organ at a reformatory chapel at the age of 14. He remembered the inmates singing "Just as I Am" and "The Old Rugged Cross."

In the middle of his critically acclaimed career as a jazz musician and composer, religious themes and motifs began to appear in his music. While composing the mass *To Hope: A Celebration*, he was so struck by the beauty and power of the liturgy that he joined the Roman Catholic Church and regularly worshiped in his parish church in Wilton, Connecticut. His funeral was celebrated in that church on December 12 and included performance of his compositions "The Desert and the Parched Land," "Psalm 23" and the "Gloria" from his mass.

I met Brubeck when he and his quartet played a magnificent concert of jazz and sacred music at Chicago's Fourth Presbyterian Church. He returned to play several times. During one of those visits he had a heart-related illness and was admitted to the hospital. Russell Gloyd, Brubeck's manager and conductor, assured me that a visit would be welcomed.

With some trepidation—as I was a bit in awe of the great artist—I went to see him. He was gracious and seemingly grateful for the visit.

We talked about music and faith, and when I asked him if I could pray with him, he immediately agreed. After that he called me his pastor. Every time he played in Chicago, my wife and I were invited to attend as his guests and to visit backstage. Without fail he would greet me with a lively "It's my pastor!" One of our dearest memories is of sharing lunch with Brubeck and his wife, Iola. In addition to being the mother of their six children, Iola was a trusted business consultant and the author of many of the lyrics to his sacred music.

At the end of my term as moderator of the 208th General Assembly of the Presbyterian Church (U.S.A.), I asked Brubeck if his quartet would play for the 209th General Assembly meeting. To my delight, he came to Syracuse and, with a local choral group, performed "All My Hope," "God's Love Made Visible" from *La Fiesta de la Posada* and the powerful "The Peace of Jerusalem" from *The Gates of Justice*. It was an evening for which I'll be forever grateful.

In every age, religion and the arts have been partners and collaborators in the great vocation of expressing human wonder and awe at the mystery of human existence and giving voice to adoration, praise and gratitude to God. Those artists include the ancient poet who wrote Psalm 96:

> Sing to the Lord, bless his name . . .
> let the earth rejoice;
> let the sea roar . . .
> let the field exult . . .
> Then shall all the trees of the forest sing for joy.

Those artists include J. S. Bach (some of whose "Jesu, Joy of Man's Desiring" occasionally emerges in the middle of a Brubeck improvisation) and Brubeck himself, who is now part of the music department, instrumental division, in the great company of heaven.

THE HISTORY CHANNEL'S VIOLENT GOD

April 2, 2013

Without intending to, I turned to the History Channel's *The Bible* recently and saw the birth of Moses, the slaughter of Hebrew babies and the rescue of baby Moses from the river. I experienced discomfort bordering on revulsion at the occasional exaggeration of the biblical narrative, yet I kept watching as Moses killed an Egyptian guard who was beating a slave and fled into the wilderness looking like Norman Mailer after a night of drinking, brawling and carousing. There he encountered Yahweh in a burning bush that reminded me of a fireworks display over Navy Pier in Chicago.

Along with millions of other viewers, I saw Moses return to the palace to confront the new pharaoh. The Passover angel of death moved through the city streets in a creeping fog that reminded me of the fog of mosquito insecticide that spewed from city trucks years ago. Then the Red Sea parted in the nick of time for the Hebrews before it flooded back to drown Pharaoh's pursuing army. There was death and destruction everywhere, all orchestrated and carried out by God.

Who could believe in a God like this? Who could believe in a God who orders his people to destroy the inhabitants of Canaan, making certain that everyone is dead, just to make way for God's people?

The problem with *The Bible* and most media representations of the biblical story is that they are so literal. In the effort to get the details of the story right, the storyteller misses the point. Over the years, most of us come to an accommodation with biblical texts that stretch the imagination—particularly those texts that portray God as vengeful, angry and murderous. We parse the Red Sea story as a myth, a story that reveals an important truth about God and human beings. Maybe the Red Sea was a swamp; maybe the pursuing Egyptian chariots became mired in the mud; maybe the people of God told the story of their ancestors' unlikely escape from Egypt and added details with each retelling. But for most of us the point is not the story; the point is the gracious providence of God, which operates in history as hope and justice and love.

Richard Rohr, a Franciscan who directs the Center for Action and Contemplation in Albuquerque, New Mexico (and writes a fine daily meditation online), offers a working hermeneutic for interpreting scripture. In regard to *any* text, Rohr proposes: "If you see God operating at a lesser level than the best person you know, then the text is not authentic revelation." If God is love (1 John 4:16), then no person could be more loving than God, Rohr says. "God is never less loving than the most loving person you know."

Most of us, like Rohr, do not believe, *cannot* believe, that God told the Hebrew people to kill everyone who got in their way. No doubt the

Hebrews did commit horrible acts; history is full of such stories. But the voice they heard wasn't God's voice.

It's a sad reality that many continue to believe that God orchestrates death, destruction and human suffering and orders people to kill. That, in my mind, is a gross and harmful distortion.

LOVABLE WINNERS?

May 11, 2015

During a recent visit to San Diego I became aware once again of the long reach of Chicago Cubs mythology. I wore my Cubs baseball cap during my daily walks and was often greeted by strangers with a smile and a "Go Cubbies!" New this spring was the comment, "This might be the year!" The mythology is rooted, of course, in the team's consistently dismal performance.

The last time the Cubs won the National League pennant and played in the World Series was 1945. The last Cubs World Series championship was in 1908—107 years ago. No other major sports franchise comes even close to that kind of futility. The Cubs are called the Lovable Losers—it's part of the myth. Preachers who know a little about baseball, and who are not averse to lacing sermons with a Cubs reference, are guaranteed to elicit knowing chuckles from congregations as far away as Dallas, New York, and New Orleans.

Everybody knows that the Cubs are a template for failure, mediocrity, and consequent despair. As such, they're a perfect metaphor for some of Christianity's most precious and potent theological themes: long suffering, patient waiting during lonely exile, hope in the face of defeat, light in the darkness, and life in the midst of death. I've turned to this rich reservoir of homiletical power regularly and shamelessly over the years.

Three weeks into the 2015 season, however, it appears that the hallowed mythology of Lovable Losers may be in serious danger. The team looks good—very good. Cubs fans are giddy with excitement at the prospect of a winning team, and maybe even contention for a championship. Now only the preachers are wary. Not only do we know about the propensity of human frailty, hubris, and sin to neutralize rosy optimism; we see the potential loss of great sermon material if the Cubs should suddenly become winners.

I am willing to pay the price. I would be more than happy to forego the references to futility and despair and indulge the prospect of a winning team.

In the foreword to Arnold Kanter's *Is God a Cubs Fan?* Rabbi Brant Rosen observes that "both baseball and Judaism are concerned with the mythic archetype of exile and return. The ultimate goal of both traditions is homecoming. In baseball players leave the safety of their dugout and run the base paths, with the hope of somehow finding their way to home plate. Likewise . . . the Jewish religion . . . maneuver[s] through the perils of exile, guided by the dream of finally returning home."

We who are Christians fully share that motif and add our own layers of meaning—the return of the Prodigal Son, for instance—and in this season of Easter we are reminded that our deepest faith is in hope gloriously realized and fulfilled in resurrection.

So maybe this is the year.

7
Civic
Engagement

WHAT STRIKES ME in this section is the wide variety of ways that Buchanan suggests mainline churches should engage with public matters in our day.

The first one, as befits the publisher of a magazine, is that we engage by informing our audience and challenging the heart, mind, and soul. The *Century* has a treasured history of doing that. John's placement of the images of Niebuhr and King in our office entryway shows this unmistakably. John actually *heard* King preach live, and he reports with awe here the enthusiasm he felt at the combination of scholarly mastery and zeal for the gospel. It's even more amazing that the *Century*'s Dean Peerman edited King ("I found him quite genial to work with"—*seriously*?!). The *Century* exemplifies here what the church believes: the communion of the saints. We're all in relationship to people we are not worthy to be related to. Baptism does amazing things.

Mainline Christians also engage in the civic sphere by voting. John has an impassioned plea for Christians not to abstain from the voting booth, illustrated by a story of Russian immigrant Jews who treated voting like the Sabbath. But then we also recognize the disappointing side of partisan politics. Sure, John gets invited to the White House, but then he gets lectured on why people of faith should vote a certain way.

Democracy is messy, fraught, and in need of statesmen and women who know how to compromise for the good of the whole.

Another way we engage is by showing an alternative form of life than the norm. The financial downturn reminds us of virtues we've long lost—of frugality, of not getting bigger than your britches. It shows us that the metastasizing of CEO pay is "grotesquely immoral," in the words of a former bank CEO. The church lives under the demands of Jesus, who asks us to give away our possessions, not to trust them, to those who genuinely need them. Perhaps the housing market meltdown and resulting world financial crises of 2008 are a reminder of the more faithful virtues of how we used to live.

The church is also a prophet and a priest. Buchanan's defense of the profound ministry of Trinity UCC in Chicago demonstrates the former, while his prayers for those affected by job loss in the economic downturn show a priestly form of civic engagement.

For the purposes of this book, Buchanan is, above all, a journalist. And the magazine's work is largely one of holding up hopeful counter-narratives to the world's dominant narrative. He found one of those in Richard Lugar, a Republican Senator from Indiana, who ignored partisan boundaries and partnered with a Democrat to drastically reduce the production and use of nuclear weapons. Buchanan praised John F. Kennedy's *Profiles in Courage* for its celebration of those who stand up for what is right, even when it is not popular. Buchanan often used his column for similar celebrations of those whose moral example in civil society is nothing short of prophetic.

THE TIME IS RIPE

January 30, 2002

In the small lobby of the offices of the *Christian Century* hang two large mounted posters. Each contains a familiar photograph of a major figure in American Christianity, along with a brief quotation from one of the articles he wrote for the *Century*. One poster features Reinhold Niebuhr; the other, Martin Luther King Jr.

King contributed to the *Century* and for a while before his death was one of our editors at large. The quotation that appears in the lobby is from the "Letter from Birmingham Jail," which appeared in the *Century* of June 12, 1963. King wrote: "Human progress never rolls in on wheels of inevitability; it comes through the tireless efforts of men [today he would add "and women"] willing to be co-workers with God, and without this hard work time itself becomes an ally of the forces of social stagnation. We must use time creatively, in the knowledge that the time is always ripe to do right."

King chose the *Century* as the journal to publish the entire letter, which he had written in response to a group of white ministers who asked him to be patient and not push the agenda of equal rights so urgently. The ministers acknowledged that his position was right, but argued that the time was not yet right. Thus King's point that "the time is always ripe to do right."

Dean Peerman, who still writes and edits for us, was the staff member who edited the letter for publication in the *Century*. He still has a copy of the original letter from the *Century*'s editor, Harold Fey, to King, acknowledging his permission and desire to have the letter published in the magazine.

As we observed King's birthday recently, I recalled my first encounter with him. He was then pastor of the Dexter Avenue Baptist Church in Montgomery, and he appeared as the guest preacher at Rockefeller Chapel at the University of Chicago. I had never heard of him before, but I was mesmerized as I listened to him preach. Here was a preacher who combined all the university criteria—he was scholarly, literate, witty—with a passionate commitment to the social, political, economic and behavioral implications of Christian faith. Here was what was missing from my experience of Christian faith—and most especially of the Christian church.

Niebuhr said somewhere that the civil rights movement saved the mainline Protestant church from irrelevance. That was my experience. It had seemed to me that believing in Jesus was a private matter—a view supported by some existentialist thought of the day. I wasn't sure that the church had anything to do with social and political concerns until I heard King and started to listen to what he was saying and watch what he was doing and to emulate, in a very modest way, what he was advocating.

Martin Luther King Jr. put the Christian faith together for me, and for that, and for the way he wove the dream of equal rights and equal justice into the soul of the culture and the church, I am forever grateful. Every time I come to work at the *Century* I see his picture, read the quote, nod in his direction and thank God for who he was and what he did.

WHITE HOUSE CHRISTIANS

November 6, 2002

I am not immune to the seduction of being invited to a White House briefing, nor of being called a "religious leader," so I flew to Washington in mid-October (at my own expense) and showed up as instructed at the Executive Office Building. There were more than a hundred of us. I recognized three Presbyterian peers, pastors of large churches. Our group included women, racial minorities and lots of young people. Someone had done some homework on the guest list.

Tim Goeglin, special assistant to the president and deputy director of the White House Office of Public Liaison, introduced the first speaker, Stephen Biegun, executive secretary of the National Security Council. Biegun, who was extraordinarily bright and articulate, works directly for Condoleezza Rice. He carefully outlined the Bush administration's assessment of international threats and then introduced a document, the National Security Strategy of the United States of America. The document asserts the U.S.'s right to take preemptive action to counter a threat to national security. That provision is obviously controversial and deserves public debate. Biegen encouraged that debate: "Read the document, debate, disagree, push back; we welcome debate," he said.

The document is available at www.whitehouse.gov, on the National Security Council page.

Then Brent Cavanaugh, associate counsel to the president, took us into the rough and tough world of national politics. The administration is very impatient with the Senate Judiciary Committee's refusal to approve President Bush's nominees for federal judgeships. Only 11 of 32 nominees have been approved and several prominent ones have been turned down. Cavanaugh began to express the administration's frustration with "liberal" political and moral values in a way that made me uncomfortable.

Jim Towey, director of the Office of Faith-Based and Community Initiatives, was next. It's hard not to like and admire him. A self-described "Pro-life Catholic Democrat," Towey worked closely with Mother Teresa and was head of Florida's Health and Social Services Agency. He is engaging, lively and passionate. "We can do better with the poor, the underserved, the sick and homeless," he says. I don't agree with him on reproductive rights, but I like him and I'm glad he's in this position. He didn't make the ideological assumptions that other speakers did.

The fourth speaker was Ken Mehlman, the White House political director and the person expected to run Bush's 2004 reelection campaign. He made it clear that in his view, our health, security and goodness as a nation depend on electing Republican candidates.

Goeglin closed the morning with the political equivalent of an altar call, asking us to go home and help elect Republican candidates in November. By this time, I was thoroughly resenting the clear assumption that a person of Christian faith will necessarily vote Republican. That attitude was very much in the air at the Executive Office Building auditorium that morning.

People of good will, integrity and honest faith can and do differ on issues of public policy, international strategy, education, tax policy. It is simply not true and not helpful to assume that the designation "liberal Democrat" captures all that is wrong and destructive of community values and national security.

My own political convictions grow out of my faith. They are often different from the political convictions of my Republican friends. It doesn't occur to me that those friends are less than faithful Christians. I would have been grateful for evidence of that same recognition on the part of the White House Office of Public Liaison.

DEMOCRATIC VIRTUE: STRADDLING THE WORLDS OF RELIGION AND POLITICS

May 4, 2004

This magazine has long straddled the world of religion and politics, convinced that political awareness and engagement are part of faithful Christian living. We do so knowing full well that this territory is highly contested. One of the ways we gauge success is by whether we get criticism from different ends of the political spectrum. That happens a lot. The right is often convinced that we are a mouthpiece for the old left. The left takes us to task for being far too soft on a range of issues.

In this issue editor-at-large Robin Lovin surveys some of the liveliest current arguments on the place of religion in democratic society and on the role particular religious commitments play in a pluralistic society. (See "Christian and Citizen".) The prominent figures in the conversation are Jeffrey Stout, Stanley Hauerwas, Alasdair MacIntyre and Richard Rorty.

I'm intrigued by Stout's vision of a secular democracy—how can there be any other kind, given our radical diversity?—as "a plurality of communities of virtue that engage with one another to order the common life." I think he's right in suggesting that the challenge before us is to live with different and in some way competing visions of what a "good society" is.

This issue will be before us in a major way in the next six months. Both presidential candidates belong to Christian churches. President Bush is a United Methodist with close ties to the evangelical world that transcends denominations. The presumptive Democratic candidate, John Kerry, is a Roman Catholic and attends mass regularly.

Interestingly, both candidates have come in conflict with church leaders—the president on the issues of Iraq and tax policy, Senator Kerry because of his positions on stem cell research and abortion. In fact, some Catholic leaders talk of denying Kerry the Eucharist because some of his positions contradict church teaching.

The first election I voted in was when John F. Kennedy was elected. I remember how concerned some people were that a Catholic president might take orders from the Vatican. I also recall Kennedy's promise to be a president who was Catholic, not a Catholic president.

This year's candidates may not read Jeffrey Stout's book, but I pray that in the days ahead they will be moved by Lovin's creative challenge:

"We have to preach virtues that in some ways set Christians at odds with their society and their neighbors, and still send them out to work with those neighbors to make society better."

CASTING MY VOTE: NOT SITTING OUT

October 5, 2004

In the previous issue, Mark Noll, a distinguished church historian, indicated his intention to sit out the upcoming presidential election because no candidate or national party reflects his sense of the pressing issues of the day ("None of the above," September 21). Noll identifies seven issues which he regards as paramount: race, respect for life, taxes, trade, medicine, religious freedom and international law. He believes that Christian faith leads him to have convictions on those issues, and I agree, though I don't share his position on all of them.

In any case, it's his conclusion not to vote that I find most provocative. To not vote? To decline to participate in what many observers think is one of the most important political choices in decades?

My summer reading included Douglas John Hall's *The Cross in Our Context*, in which Hall, in the spirit of Dietrich Bonhoeffer and Reinhold Niebuhr, declares that we are called to live in this world. The cross speaks of God's passionate and complete love for this fallen creation. Pay attention to the world, Hall urges. The church's task is to be as thoroughly in the world as its crucified Lord was. Never, never abandon the world. Given that understanding, I wonder if one can avoid involving oneself in the messy choices of politics.

I'm involved in several conversations in Chicago between Jews and Christians about difficult issues, including Israel/Palestine and this magazine's coverage of that conflict. Out of these conversations has come a precious friendship with Rabbi Yehiel Poupko, a Judaic scholar at the Chicago branch of the American Jewish Federation. He recently told me about his grandparents, who came to this country from Russia. He also told me that when his grandmother learned that he had decided to sit out the 1968 election because of his dissatisfaction with both candidates, she telephoned him in rabbinical school and said to him in Yiddish: "Your grandfather and I suffered under the czars and then we suffered under Lenin and Stalin. We never had the right to vote, and you're going to now sit out an election and not vote?"

Rabbi Poupko recalled how his grandparents would dress up in their Sabbath best to go to the polls, thrilled to live in a place where their vote counted. "They were always the first ones there, early in the morning. This is a remarkable place. None of our people have ever lived in a place like this in the past 2,000 years."

For me, the thought of that elderly Jewish couple standing outside the polling place at dawn in their Sabbath clothes is another encouragement to jump into this troubled, fallen world and cast a vote.

HEALTHY LIMITS: ON THE IMPORTANCE OF FAITH AND THE DANGERS OF EXTREMISM

August 8, 2006

On the heels of denominational meetings this summer, "Everything you wanted to know about Christianity," by Dennis Colby, is just what I needed. I take my denominational responsibilities seriously. I value the theological traditions. I attend the meetings, serve on the committees and engage in the debates. Sometimes what the enterprise needs most is a little humor, a little of the laughter that God must indulge in when human beings take themselves too seriously. Only people who are secure can laugh at themselves and poke fun at their own foibles.

A healthy sense of human limits is an important feature of political engagement too, as David Heim suggests in his article on the religious left ("Christian and Citizen"). A similar point is made by former secretary of state Madeleine Albright in her book about religion and statesmanship, *The Mighty and the Almighty: Reflections on America, God, and World Affairs.* "We would be well advised," she writes, "to recall the character of wartime leadership provided by Abraham Lincoln. He did not flinch from fighting in a just cause, but he never claimed a monopoly on virtue. . . . He rejected the suggestion that he pray for God to be on the side of the Union, praying instead for the Union to be on God's side."

Another helpful book on religion and politics is Jon Meacham's *American Gospel: God, the Founding Fathers, and the Making of a*

Nation. Meacham argues that the founders understood the importance of religious faith in the political arena but also knew about the dangers of religious extremism and absolutism.

When the founders gathered for the inaugural session of the Continental Congress in 1774, their first fight was about religion. Thomas Cushing of Massachusetts wanted to begin with prayer. John Jay and John Rutledge objected. Samuel Adams proposed a compromise. Meacham observes that the founders could have ruled out all religion and created a totally secular state. They didn't choose that route because they understood how important religious faith is for the formation of values and for the well-being of society and government. But they also understood how religion can be used to malign and divide.

The majority of the founders were Christians, although they exhibited considerable theological diversity. They agreed on the importance of the freedom of religion—not knowing how this principle would eventually lead to a nation of great religious diversity. Meacham reports that when the U.S. made a treaty with the Muslim state of Tripoli in 1797, "the Founders declared that 'the Government of the United States is not in any way founded on the Christian Religion.'" There's something to bring up the next time you hear someone argue that the nation is a Christian republic.

HARD WORDS: WRIGHT'S JEREMIAD

April 22, 2008

I wish Jeremiah Wright had made his point about America's failings without saying "God damn America." But not for a moment do I wish he had been less prophetic. The great biblical prophets did and said outrageous, controversial things, which consistently got them in trouble and occasionally landed them in jail. I wish Wright had not said "America's chickens are coming home to roost" about the terrorist attacks on September 11, 2001. But he claimed to be paraphrasing a commentator on TV who—quite reasonably—had pointed out objectionable and self-defeating U.S. foreign policies.

Critics of Wright and Barack Obama wonder how Senator Obama could have remained in Wright's congregation for 20 years. The answer is that Wright didn't say "God damn America" every Sunday. Wright's sermons, week after week, were biblically based, relevant, literate and eloquent. When preachers of the land think about whose sermons and lectures they want to hear, Wright's name is near the top of the list.

With cable TV shows playing a few sound bites of Wright over and over again, it's no wonder people who don't know a thing about Trinity United Church of Christ or Jeremiah Wright come to the wrong conclusions. I'm not the only preacher in the land who knows how vulnerable any one of us is should some ill-chosen words be lifted out of a sermon to be replayed over and over.

Wright and Trinity Church should be put in the context of the church's entire ministry. Under Wright's leadership, Trinity reached out to the community with mission programs, education, social services, AIDS education and treatment programs and health care. Driving on Stony Island Avenue on Chicago's far South Side, you pass by a large community health center sponsored by Trinity. One way to evaluate and measure a ministry is by the mission it performs. Among Chicago churches and Chicago clergy of all denominations, Trinity is widely admired as a model of what a public church can and ought to be.

Katharine Moon, a professor of political science at Wellesley and a Korean American, recently remembered the church in which she was nurtured and reminded us all of the special role congregations play:

> Churches, synagogues, mosques, prayer meetings are . . . communities of mutual help, support and practical guidance. As social scientists know, they are instrumental to building and maintaining social capital. For new immigrants, as well as racial and ethnic minorities, they serve a particular purpose. Often, the immigrant or ethnic church is the one public place where a common language, food and humor particular to one's cultural heritage can be shared. . . . It is through the congregation that we ask for help—to look after our children or elderly parents. . . . Often it is the people in the worship hall who . . . help us paint our houses, and visit us in hospitals. . . . A house of worship is much more than a pastor. (*Chicago Tribune*, March 25)[1]

Those sensible, valuable words should help us think more clearly about pastors and congregations, and about what it means to be a member of a congregation—even if one happens to be a candidate for president.

WILDERNESS OF UNCERTAINTY:
FORGOTTEN VIRTUES TO RELEARN

April 7, 2009

Theologian N. T. Wright says that even when you are in the Promised Land you are never far from the wilderness. I'm not the only preacher who has pondered how our nation has gone so quickly from the promised land of abundance to a wilderness of economic uncertainty. This recession is a new place for most of us. We had come to assume uninterrupted economic growth and the safety and stability of our investments and of the institutions we treasure and support—churches, seminaries, colleges, hospitals.

I do not believe that God is in the business of correcting a misdirected global economy. But because I am a Christian, I do believe that God comes into the wilderness, and because of that I believe there are always redemptive outcomes and things to learn. No good, of course, comes from losing your home, your job, your health insurance. But God can make something good happen in the midst of bad circumstances. Maybe what this crisis can teach us is the relative value of things, the true value of what you treasure most.

A member of my congregation sent me two articles on the economy recently. One was tongue-in-cheek, "20 Things that Won't Survive the Crisis"[2]—funny in a painful way. What won't survive: "your 401(k)," for instance. And the Hummer. "The Chinese will probably buy Hummers and make a fortune selling them as mobile homes."

The other piece was "13 Unexpected Consequences of the Financial Crisis,"[3] one of which is that our children will learn from our Depression-era parents, not from us, to be savers. It reminded me that I grew up in a happy, modest home which by the standards to which I have become accustomed was poor, but we didn't know it. It reminded me that my father, who became an adult in the Depression, never owned a credit card and never understood the logic of paying interest to fill your tank with gas.

The late Tim Russert, host of NBC's *Meet the Press*, wrote a delightful book about his father, *Big Russ and Me*. His father was a modest man who worked hard and raised his family in a blue-collar neighborhood of South Buffalo and was always admired and respected by his many friends. Big Russ loved cars, but he drove used cars and said that someday he'd like to own a new Cadillac. Tim used to say that someday he'd buy his dad a brand new Cadillac.

Before his father's 75th birthday, Russert, now very successful, called his dad and said, "OK, I'm finally in a position to buy you a new car. When I come home for Thanksgiving we'll pick it up." He sent his father catalogs for Cadillac, Mercedes and Lexus cars: "You can have any car you want, with options."

When he came home for the holiday, Russert and his father drove to pick up the new car his father had chosen—a black Ford Crown Victoria. "Dad—it's a cop car."

On the drive home Tim had to ask: "When I was a kid you always said you wanted a Cadillac. Why the Ford?" His father's answer: "Do I think it's a better car? No. But if I came home with a fancy Cadillac, do you know what people would say?" 'What happened to Tim [Sr.]? He's got too big for us. His kid makes it big and now he's driving a Cadillac.' No, I can't do that. This is what I want. This is who I am."

If there is anything redemptive about this crisis, it is the possibility it offers to learn again the virtues we may have forgotten—modesty, frugality, responsibility, community—and to learn again who we are.

GROSS INEQUITY

November 4, 2011

When the *Chicago Tribune* asked Rahm Emanuel about the Chicago version of Occupy Wall Street, the mayor of Chicago said that although he did not agree with some of the tactics and proposals of the protesters, no one could ignore the fact that many Americans live on the edge of financial disaster. "If you can't hear the anguish in people's lives," he said, "you're too callous for public life."[4]

This issue of the *Century* includes Gary Dorrien's essay "The case against Wall Street." Not everyone will agree with Dorrien's analysis or proposals. When I asked a New York banker about the situation, he pointed out that if the government had not bailed out the banks, the entire banking system might have collapsed. Automakers avoided total collapse and are back on their feet thanks to government financial support. Americans who might otherwise be unemployed have jobs and incomes thanks to millions of dollars of infrastructure support. My banker friend suggested that the real problem is money in politics and that the number one economic challenge is meaningful tax reform.

Setting our financial house in order is a moral as well as a political and economic matter. As Dorrien observes, the top 10 percent of the American people hold more than 70 percent of the wealth. Historians warn that the growing gap is not sustainable and is likely to result in catastrophe.

I had the pleasure of knowing William J. McDonough, who at one time was CEO of one of Chicago's largest banks. After the Enron accounting scandal and the collapse of the corporation as a result of executive mismanagement and deception, McDonough left banking and became chairman of the Public Company Accounting Oversight Board. In an address titled "The Challenge for Private Sector Leaders," McDonough said that the accounting scandals of the 1990s happened because "many American business leaders got confused and their moral compasses stopped working."

Then, in front of a gathering of Chicago's business and corporate leaders, he addressed the topic of executive compensation. "In 1980, the average large company chief executive officer made 40 times more than the average employee in his or her firm." By 2000, the multiple had risen to at least 400 times. In other words, over the course of 20 years, the CEO pay multiple went up by about 1,000 percent. "There is no economic theory, however farfetched, which can justify that increase," said McDonough. "It is also grotesquely immoral." These would be strong words coming from a theology professor or preacher. They came from a former bank CEO.

The economic crisis hits home to me every week during our church's staff meeting, when we take time to create a list of pastoral concerns: hospitalizations, illnesses and deaths. We discuss each concern and assign someone to follow up. Recently we've added a new category: job loss and unemployment. Our staff's weekly check-in time reminds me that these are urgent matters—and that we must have a solution. Reaching one is likely to require political courage.

COURAGE TO COMPROMISE

June 26, 2012

On a steamy summer afternoon in the 1970s, Richard Lugar came to Hanover College in southern Indiana to speak at a synod meeting about politics as a sacred calling and about how his faith and church membership were an important part of his vocation. Lugar was first elected to the U.S. Senate in 1976 after two terms as mayor of Indianapolis. He had gained national recognition for Unigov, a consolidation of the Indianapolis and Marion County governments that is credited with stimulating Indianapolis's impressive economic growth.

As a young pastor in northern Indiana, I was deeply impressed, and reminded of John F. Kennedy's words about the importance and dignity of the political vocation. I was proud of Lugar, a Republican, and of Democratic senator Birch Bayh, both of whom had reputations as moderates who collaborated with senators from the other party.

One of Lugar's crowning achievements was collaborating with Sam Nunn, a Democrat, to reduce the use, production and stockpiling of nuclear, chemical and biological weapons. Today the Nunn-Lugar Cooperative Threat Reduction Program has deactivated more than 7,500 nuclear warheads. Lugar also cooperated with then senator Joe Biden on complex Pakistani issues and traveled to Russia with then senator Barack Obama.

I was sorry when Lugar lost his recent primary race to state treasurer Richard Mourdock. The race wasn't even close. Lugar's age was a factor, as were questions about his residency. But the major reason for his defeat was that the Tea Party and conservative Super PACs such as Freedom Works and Club for Growth poured cash into the Mourdock campaign for the express purpose of replacing Lugar's brand of moderate bipartisanship with more ideologically orthodox conservatism.

Lugar wrote a letter afterward, affirming his continuing loyalty to the Republican Party and his commitment to working for Mourdock's election. Then he offered some advice. Mourdock had attacked Lugar's brand of Republicanism, saying that "it's time for confrontation, not collaboration." Lugar wrote that Mourdock will have to revise his unrelenting partisanship if he is to be an effective senator. The effort to cleanse the party of any who deviate from conservative orthodoxy will only magnify the seriousness of the issues facing the nation. "There is little likelihood that either party will be able to impose their favored budget solutions on the other without some degree of compromise."

Then Lugar revealed his deepest convictions: "Legislators should have an ideological grounding and strong beliefs. . . . But ideology cannot be a substitute for a determination to think for yourself, a willingness to study an issue objectively, and for the fortitude to sometimes disagree with your party or even your constituents."

Lugar symbolizes something great but fragile about the American system of government: it relies on partisanship tempered by wisdom, on a commitment to the good of the nation that is not wedded to ideology. It is the genius of our system that people with deeply held and opposing ideas can clash yet still find ways to collaborate.

JFK's *Profiles in Courage*, written in 1955, influenced me deeply. It is about a handful of Americans who, at critical moments, made decisions that departed from their parties' ideologies, confounded their own supporters and ultimately cost them dearly. It discusses John Quincy Adams, who was removed from his Senate seat for supporting an embargo on British goods that hurt his New England merchant constituents. JFK also notes the case of Robert Taft, the staunchly conservative Republican senator from Ohio who publicly opposed the Nuremberg Trials after World War II. "The trial of the vanquished by the victor cannot be impartial no matter how it is hedged about with the forms of justice," Taft warned. Almost nobody agreed with Taft after the horrors of the Nazi era; his position may have cost him his party's presidential nomination in 1948.

Kennedy named it courage, the willingness to do and say what one thinks is the right thing regardless of consequences. Lugar had it.

RELIGION AND POLITICS DO MIX

July 20, 2015

The conventional maxim "religion and politics do not and should not mix" is not only wrong but misleading and downright silly. Of course religion and politics mix. Our deepest values are often rooted in our religious beliefs and inform how we live, how we order our priorities, how we spend our time and money, and how we vote.

What this statement really means is that *"your* religion and *my* politics don't mix." The maxim is often confused with the separation of church and state. The founders of the nation decided that the new republic would not have a state religion and an established state church. Citizens would enjoy a completely new phenomenon: freedom of religion and freedom to believe or not believe, to belong to a church or not, according to the dictates of one's own conscience. No one thought it would work. How can a state survive without religious support? How can a church survive without state sponsorship?

The wall separating church and state is mentioned not in the Constitution per se, but in a letter that Thomas Jefferson addressed to some concerned Baptists in Connecticut. One effect of the letter was to encourage citizens to seek civic and political involvement as an expression of their religion and to assume responsibility for their churches. American churches have been doing this—expressing their convictions with political ramifications—all the way back to colonial days when American Presbyterians, at their first General Assembly, addressed themselves to President George Washington.

Now Pope Francis has delivered his encyclical *Laudato Si.* He chose words from St. Francis of Assisi's "Canticle to the Sun," a poem that praises the Creator for the gift of the creation and assumes human responsibility for it. Using blunt language, the pope observed that we human beings have made a mess of things. He invoked scientific data to support his point and named climate change and global warming as major threats to all of us.

William Schweiker of the University of Chicago Divinity School observed that even before *Laudato Si* was officially released, critics lined up to dispute the pope and to question not only his scientific credentials but also the appropriateness of the pope addressing an issue with huge economic and political implications. Catholic Republican presidential candidates scrambled to find a way to appease a conservative base that denies human involvement in climate change while not publicly disagreeing with the pope. Jeb Bush, a convert to Roman Catholicism, said he doesn't get his economic policy from bishops and the pope. He elaborated: "I think religion ought to be about making us better people and less about things that end up getting us into the political realm"—that is, religion and politics don't mix.

But they do: we want better health care and education for everyone because neighbor love is one of our deepest values and commitments. We want safe food, safe automobiles, and a judicial system that guarantees equal treatment for all. And we want a sustainable environment for our grandchildren.

The pope broke new ground, Schweiker points out, by unapologetically using current science to back up his claim about human involvement and by reminding us that religious conviction and scientific inquiry cannot and ought not be at cross purposes on critical public issues.

The pope also reminded us that the first and most severely affected victims of climate change are the poor and marginalized of every nation. Affluence insulates some of us. Some of us can purchase bigger air conditioners and move to cooler climes if necessary. But most of the people of the world cannot.

Whatever Protestant misgivings I have about the papacy, Francis, on this issue, is my pope.

8
The
Middle East

THERE IS A TONE of sadness, anger, or even despair in some of these essays, a tone that increases as time goes along. John Buchanan has been a leader in the Presbyterian Church and has tried to help guide that body he loves to discuss and interact with Israel in ways that are not self-defeating. The church's recent vote for divestment, chronicled in the final essay here, went another way from the conscientious bridge-building Buchanan has long tried to cultivate.

The issues here are "messy," to employ one of John's favorite terms—messier even than normal politics. They involve three religions, of which ours is the least consequential in the conversation. They involve a history of Christian anti-Judaism from which we are still trying to recover. They involve new pressures in the form of Christian premillenialist support for Israel on the way to a particular end-times scenario which is not good news for Jews (but if you're Jewish and think the fundamentalists' apocalypse is not going to happen anyway, why worry?). It involves decreasing strength in mainline churches—as we lose power we seem more inclined to kick left in increasingly empty anti-Israel gestures. It involves increasing strength of extremists both among Israelis and Palestinians. As the indigenous Christian presence in the Middle East shrinks to nothing, mainline churches' role and voice may decrease still more. Left to our own devices, we may well be through here.

But we are not left to our own devices. Some of these essays call for traditional practices of the Abrahamic faith that could—who knows?—make a way where there is now no way. We should weep together. When violence claims a child or neighborhood, our first response shouldn't be vengeance but sorrow. We should pray together. "Pray for the peace of Jerusalem," the psalmist says, in one of the few directives to which all sides agree. We can name things truthfully. These essays detail specific events and patterns of behavior that shouldn't be repeated: indiscriminate civilian targeting and quite intentionally destabilizing settlement building. We can hope. It's not hope if things look rosy. That's just optimism. Hope sees the realities John names and sees a God who promises new realities.

Rowan Williams often speaks of the gospel making things *difficult*. Here we might say things are difficult enough already! Americans who travel to the Middle East are often staggered at the length of memories and the multiple entanglements no one could unravel. We Americans are impatient with complexity. But these essays show this area is not going for any simple solution any time soon. Perhaps some state actor other than America will do better than we have arbitrating this thing— our optimism and lack of memory seem not to have served us well in our brokering role.

I'm haunted by John's comment that Presbyterians have experienced no pogroms. One dream of America's settlers was not to have their lives determined any longer by memories too long and grievances too eagerly nurtured. In the Middle East, we plunge into memories both longer than Europe's and more deeply and recently pained than anything we mainline Protestants have experienced. Are we American Christians the right ones to be weighing in here? Were we ever?

More hauntingly still: Who else is there?

ESTRANGED: BETWEEN MAINLINE
PROTESTANTS AND JEWS

June 28, 2003

A painful accompaniment to the conflict between Israel and the Palestinians is the estrangement it has caused between mainline Protestants and Jews. For decades mainline Protestants have fostered theological dialogue with the Jewish community. Christian and Jewish scholars have worked together on common texts and common history. No seminary education is complete without reading works by Rabbi Joshua Abraham Heschel. Christian and Jewish congregations have studied, worked and worshiped together in a way that has fostered a new climate of understanding and mutual affirmation. The Presbyterian congregation I serve is honored to host Rosh Hashanah and Yom Kippur High Holiday services for neighboring Congregation Sinai. That congregation, in turn, allows us to use its facilities for retreats and conferences, and every Lent its people help us understand their Seder tradition and its relationship to Jesus' last supper.

But now we find ourselves in a difficult place. Mainline Protestant denominations have been sympathetic to the aspirations of the Palestinian people for an independent nation, and they have sometimes been critical of Israel's policies. And that stance has been hurtful to our Jewish friends. Most troubling of all has been the fact that some Jews have regarded Christian expressions of support for the Palestinian cause and of opposition to Israeli policies as a form of anti-Semitism.

No Christian who knows how anti-Semitism grew and thrived in the bosom of Christianity is anything but appalled by the unprecedented evil of the Holocaust. Christians are also appalled by suicide bombings which take the lives of innocent Israeli citizens. Those deeds underscore the absolute necessity of a strong and secure state of Israel. Most mainline Christians, I believe, pray for that and, at the same time, for an independent, viable and secure Palestinian state. And we also pray for the occasion to join hands again with Jews, working together for justice and peace.

An additional twist in this estrangement is the burgeoning alliance between premillenialist fundamentalist Christians and Israel, which Donald Wagner ("Marching to Zion") describes in this issue. Israelis are understandably happy for the support. But it is dismaying and ironic that those Christians who believe Israel has a biblical claim on the land are the ones who see Israel's future as merely a prelude to the end of the Jewish faith. As historian Martin Marty recently observed to Jewish colleagues, "The fundamentalists/premillennialists cast you in the first act of a two-act drama, but you are not part of the second act."

A far better conversation is the one Protestants and Jews were formerly embarked upon: about the nature of God's covenant, how Christians and Jews relate to one another as people of the covenant, and how Christians can pay more attention to the bonds of history and faith which Jews and Christians share and which are God's gifts to us.

FAMILY TENSIONS: THE PCUSA AND PALESTINE

November 16, 2004

Last summer the General Assembly of the Presbyterian Church (U.S.A.) passed several resolutions that have distressed the American Jewish community. The church criticized Israeli policy toward Palestinians, condemned Israel's construction of a security barrier, declined to withdraw support for a congregation in Philadelphia which appears to target Jews for conversion and—the move that most angered the Jewish community—voted to consider selective divestment from corporations that do business in Israel.

Some Jews interpreted the action as an attack on Israel—perhaps even an anti-Semitic gesture. Presbyterians have been stunned by the depth of Jewish anger, and how what seems to many like legitimate social witness is experienced as a form of anti-Semitism.

Then, when it seemed like things could not become worse, they did. A Presbyterian delegation visiting the Middle East met with representatives of Hezbollah, an Islamic organization which the U.S. Council on Foreign Relations says has "planned and has links to" international terrorist activities. After the conversation, one of the Presbyterian participants told the press that "relations and conversations with Islamic leaders are a lot easier than dealings and dialogue with Jewish leaders." The comment was broadcast widely in the Arab media. The individual who made the comment was not a spokesperson for the PCUSA or the delegation. Church officials immediately called the comments "reprehensible" and not reflective of the PCUSA. They also called the unauthorized visit "misguided at best."

No doubt the PCUSA's orderly polity will be used to sort things out. My guess is that Presbyterians will have an intense conversation about divestment as a method of social witness and about unauthorized meetings involving Presbyterian delegations. I hope we will reaffirm our position that while everyone is welcome in our churches and God's love in Jesus Christ is for all, our brothers and sisters of the Covenant are not objects for proselytizing.

A recent visit to the Gettysburg battlefield reminded me that family fights are often the most tragic and horrific. My hope is that Christians will join with Jews in some intentional listening to one another, exercise the forbearance and forgiveness which lie at the heart of our shared tradition and maybe even reenergize the collaboration which is precious to both our traditions.

A starting point might be a joint reading of *The Dignity of Difference*, by Jonathan Sacks, the chief rabbi in Great Britain. He caught my attention with these opening words: "I see in the rising crescendo of ethnic tensions, civilization clashes and the use of religious justification for acts of terror, a clear and present danger to humanity. For too long the pages of history have been stained by blood shed in the name of God . . . In our interconnected world, we must learn to feel enlarged, not threatened, by difference."

INVESTED INTERESTS: DIVESTMENT STRATEGY

December 28, 2004

The prophet Isaiah, whose words we read in Advent, gives us wonderful images of peace and of the restoration of Zion—images of the wolf living with the lamb, of waters breaking forth out of the wilderness, of a land where there shall be "no lion, nor any ravenous beast."

I can't read these passages, however, without remembering Woody Allen's comment that when lion and calf lie down together, only the lion will get back up. I also recall something Dietrich Bonhoeffer said about peace being the opposite of security—peace is a great venture, something to be dared.

The General Assembly of the Presbyterian Church (U.S.A.) recently made what it thought was a daring decision on behalf of peace. It decided to begin a process of selected, phased divestment from corporations whose business is deemed harmful to Palestinians and Israelis. The response to this decision inside and outside Presbyterian congregations has been vigorous and heated—and not exactly peaceful.

Our Jewish neighbors have been deeply hurt by what they regard as an attack on the state of Israel and its economy, and on Jews personally. I have tried to interpret my church's action to Jewish friends by explaining that its focus is Israeli policy, not Israel's economy or existence and certainly not Jewish people.

I have also tried to help congregation members, who aren't always paying attention to what their denomination is doing, or who wonder why it is doing what it does, to provide some answers when their Jewish neighbors or co-workers ask them why the Presbyterian Church is picking on Israel.

Is there a way to show that the church's concern is truly for peace? The congregation I serve took up this question, and after much discussion it came up with a strategy. The session produced a statement that, among other things:

— Asks the PCUSA to slow the divestment process in order to give the Jewish and Palestinian communities an opportunity to be heard.
— Asks the denomination, should divestment ultimately happen, to reinvest whatever proceeds are realized from the sale of divested holdings in corporations whose business in Israel is deemed positive, helpful and peaceful.
— Instructs its own investment committee to invest some funds in those kinds of businesses in order to underscore that the target is not Israel's existence.

The statement also expresses the belief, so central to those Isaiah passages and the faith tradition of Jews, Muslims and Christians, that finding a way to work together is the best hope for peace in a land that is precious to us all.

CONSEQUENCES: THE LASTING EFFECTS OF 9/11

October 16, 2007

On the sixth anniversary of 9/11 I joined a spokesperson for the American Muslim community on a panel focusing on the lasting effects of 9/11 on "faith, media and society." The presentation by Imam A. Malik Mujahid, chair of the Council of Islamic Organizations of Greater Chicago, was illuminating—and discomforting.

He began by saying that there is now a Sixth Pillar of Islam for American Muslims: "Thou shalt condemn terrorism five times a day." Mujahid pointed out that Muslim leaders here and abroad have condemned the 9/11 attacks and other suicide bombings, but the press simply doesn't pay attention.

He reported that life has become increasingly difficult for Muslims living in the U.S. A Pew Forum survey revealed that 70 percent of Americans say that Islam has little or nothing in common with their own religion, and 45 percent believe that Islam encourages violence. He said 500,000 Muslims were interviewed by the FBI after 9/11 (25 percent of all Muslim households); 28,000 Muslims were detained, many in special prisons built for the purpose; but only 39 Muslims have been charged or convicted.

Mujahid told about preaching in a mosque in Pakistan—he is a native Pakistani—shortly after the murder of American journalist Daniel Pearl by extremists. He spoke about Pearl's career, family and values. There were, he said, many tears and much sympathy among the Islamic congregants.

Muslims understand—better than we Christians do, I think—the tragic, deadly convergence between Islamic fundamentalism and a violent political ideology. They ask simply that we be fair and informed in our assessments. On the situation in Iraq, Mujahid suggested that Americans should remember that Iraq has often been invaded and occupied by Western military powers, and that Iraqi conventional wisdom holds that the goal is always Iraqi oil.

Mujahid and other Muslim leaders are under no illusions about what may happen if American and coalition forces withdraw from Iraq, but he thinks that the U.S. presence is making matters worse. That's a conclusion to which many Americans have come—including Melvin Laird, who was secretary of defense in the Nixon administration. Laird wrote in *Foreign Affairs*, "Our presence is what feeds the insurgency."

A NEW YEAR'S PROMISE: BREAKING
THE MIDDLE EAST DEADLOCK

January 13, 2009

A new administration in Washington brings the promise of new approaches to deadlocked and dangerous international conflicts. President-elect Obama has indicated his intent to rethink and recast our relationship with Cuba, for instance. Anyone who visits Cuba can see how the U.S. boycott and effort to isolate the Castro regime has provided Cuban leaders with a convenient villain on whom to blame Cuba's weak economy and daily hardships.

A new administration can also bring fresh approaches to the Israel-Palestine conflict, leading to the end that everyone knows is necessary—a viable and secure Palestinian state alongside a viable and secure Israel.

This issue features an exchange on the biblical promise of land to the Jews, with Gary Anderson arguing that Christians cannot simply ignore this promise ("Does the Promise Still Hold?: Israel and the Land"). Nor can Christians ignore readings like this one, which the lectionary assigns for the fourth Sunday in Advent, from 2 Samuel 7: "And I will appoint a place for my people Israel and will plant them, so that they may live in their own place, and be disturbed no more; and evildoers shall afflict them no more, as formerly, from the time that I appointed judges over my people Israel; and I will give you rest from your enemies."

It took a long process for me to begin to understand the importance of the land of Israel to my Jewish friends. When my denomination voted several years ago to divest itself from corporations whose business in Israel is deemed harmful to Palestinian people, a firestorm of angry protest erupted in my community and throughout the country. Many Jewish leaders interpreted divestment as an attack on the economy of Israel and thus an attack on the very existence of Israel. Like many others, I was astonished that what many of us thought was a critique of particular Israeli policies was experienced as an attack on Israel's right to exist.

In response to that debate, a small group of Jewish and Christian scholars, clergy and laity met regularly in Chicago. The conversations were open, honest, sometimes angry. Our Jewish partners wondered why mainline Protestants were outspoken on Israel's human rights violations and relatively silent about the behavior of states like Cuba, North Korea and China. Our response, not universally accepted, was that we were critical precisely because Israel is a democracy and a close ally, and because our expectations are higher for Israel than for less democratic states or for states that do not receive military aid from the U.S.

What I took away from the experience mostly was a new appreciation for what the land and the state of Israel mean to my Jewish friends. There is simply no equivalence in the religious experience of most Christians. Most of us never had a land that was very important to our identity and our religion. Presbyterians never have had pogroms aimed at us; we were never ghettoized, discriminated against or kept out of clubs, universities and law practices because of being Presbyterian. There is no Holocaust in our religious experience.

I'm praying for new American leadership in the Middle East, a breakthrough in peace negotiations, and renewed conversations among Christians and between Jews and Christians about the land, the Bible and our hopes for peace.

TOUGH CONVERSATIONS

September 7, 2011

Last month, in an essay in the *New York Times,* columnist Roger Cohen cited an American protagonist in a Philip Roth novel who said that "in England, when someone mentions the word 'Jew,' I notice that the voice always drops a little."[1] Anti-Semitism is always just beneath the surface in England, Cohen observed. Conventional stereotypes can surface in genteel conversation.

Cohen then explored another minefield of identity: he related how in the U.S. he has been accused by other Jews of not being a real Jew or of being a "self-hating Jew," because he has criticized Israel for what he calls its "self-defeating expansion of settlements in the West Bank." His essay—and the critical response he received—is one sign of how difficult it is for Jews to talk about the Israeli-Palestinian conflict.

It is also difficult for Christians to talk about it with Jews. In August, Glenn Beck, the former Fox News talk-show host, toured Israel and held a "Restoring Courage" rally in Jerusalem. His aim was to display American solidarity with Israel. Beck's visit was embraced by some Israelis, who are eager for such expressions of support, and reviled by other Israelis, who noted Beck's penchant for anti-Semitic outbursts and extreme anti-Muslim rhetoric. "If this is the only kind of friend Israel's government can find around the world, that's a very poor sign," said Yariv Oppenheimer, secretary-general of Peace Now.[2]

Mainline Christians often wonder about Israelis' willingness to embrace people like Beck as well as fundamentalist Christians who support the state of Israel because they believe it has a role in the end times, in which Jews will be converted to Christ. I was once part of a Jewish-Christian dialogue group in which that issue was raised: "Surely," one Christian said to the Jewish participants, "you know that those Christians support you because you are instrumental in their hope for the return of Christ—but you are not part of the last chapter in their story." An official of a Jewish organization assured us that Jews understand Christian premillennialist thinking, but said that when Jews feel under siege and feel that their old friends, the mainline Protestant denominations, have turned against them, they are glad to get support, regardless of the source.

Talking together about the things that make for peace is difficult, but Christians and Jews must keep at it. That is part of our identity. Christians and Jews share a commitment to peace and justice. Together we must pray that some game-changing event will occur, that Israelis and Palestinians will each take political risks for the sake of peace. A section in my church's book of Confessions of Faith says that "the church, in its own life, is called to practice the forgiveness of enemies and to commend to the nations as practical politics the search for cooperation and peace. This search requires that the nations pursue fresh and responsible relations across every line of conflict, even at risk to national security" (Confession of 1967).

INVESTING IN PALESTINIANS

May 2, 2012

How can the churches acknowledge the complexity of the political challenges in the Middle East? How can Christians support Palestinian brothers and sisters in faith who are caught in that complexity and have endured four decades of Israeli occupation and restricted human rights? And how do we respond in a way that actually helps Israelis and Palestinians move toward peace and mutual security?

One response is the so-called BDS movement, which has proposed boycotts, divestment and sanctions from corporations that do business with Israel and are deemed harmful to the prospects for peace and harmful to Palestinians and which has publicly condemned Israel as an "apartheid" state.

In this issue ("Investment, not divestment"), Thomas A. Prinz and Karl-John N. Stone argue for an alternate response—positive investment in the Palestinian economy. In 2010, *New York Times* columnist Thomas Friedman argued that a viable Palestinian state (which a majority of Israelis support) must have strong Palestinian institutions and businesses and that the best way to further that goal is to invest in those institutions and businesses. He commended Palestinian prime minister Salam Fayyad, a former World Bank economist who has "unleashed the real Palestinian revolution" with his efforts to build a viable economy and market.

Although I have friends who are committed to the BDS movement, I find it difficult to agree with them. I am fairly certain that the decision of an American denomination to divest has no effect on Israeli policy and no effect on the corporations involved. BDS adds to Israel's sense of isolation and perplexes and angers American Jews.

A rabbi who is a vocal critic of the current Israeli government and a strong advocate for Palestinians' rights made this point to me: "When you Christians start talking about divesting from Israel, it sounds to us as if you are undermining Israel's economy and thus Israel's existence. We close ranks, and even progressive, sympathetic Jews become adamant Zionists."

In a controversial new book, *The Crisis in Zionism,* Peter Beinart laments the continuing Israeli occupation of Palestinian territories, the failure to establish an independent Palestinian state, and the ongoing expansion of Israeli settlements in land needed for such a state. The situation is not only immoral and unjust, says Beinart, but seriously compromises and endangers core Israeli values of democracy and human rights. Yet Beinart also argues that comparing the BDS effort to the "global antiapartheid struggle sends the message that just as the apartheid state in South Africa was dismantled, so must the Jewish state be dismantled today." Beinart proposes instead a boycott of illegal settlements and the goods they produce.

Beinart's book will make many American Jews and Christians

uncomfortable—the *New York Times* reviewer said it is filled with "Manichaean simplicities"[3]—but as Bill Clinton wrote, "Beinart raises the tough questions that can't be avoided, and offers a new way forward to achieve Zionism's founding ideals."

I'm hoping for positive investment in Palestine by denominations, congregations and individuals, Christian and Jewish. I'm hoping for one thing more: that every Christian congregation will sit down with a neighboring synagogue to talk about what is happening in Israel/Palestine and why each of us cares about it.

WEEP TOGETHER

May 8, 2014

The Middle East peace talks appear to be at a dead end. At the last minute Israel reneged on a promise to release Palestinian prisoners and announced the construction of yet more housing in territory claimed by the Palestinians for a future state. The Palestinians responded by applying for membership in United Nations agencies—something both Israel and the United States have requested they not do. Each side blames the other for the failure of the peace process. Yet it does not seem that either side truly wants a resolution, even though the continuation of the status quo will lead to a disaster for both sides. In the meantime, most likely as an expression of frustration and desperation, the boycott, divestment, and sanctions movement against Israel is gaining momentum.

Recently, in the space of a few days, the editorial staff of the *Century* met with a Palestinian Christian leader and a Chicago rabbi who works for a major national Jewish organization. Both men are friends of mine, as well as distinguished clergy and respected leaders.

After engaging in conversation with them, I was struck once again by the conflicting narratives: how the same events in the same period of time and the same place sound entirely different depending on who's telling the story. It's somewhat like the American story—told one way by European settlers and their descendants and another way by Native Americans and their descendants.

One visitor represented the narrative of a people subjected to a millennium and a half of relentless persecution: expelled from homes, confined behind ghetto walls, and nearly obliterated in state-conducted genocide. Finally, with UN approval, they claimed a nation state in a place where their ancestors had lived centuries before. The other visitor's narrative was about a people who were violently displaced from their land and pushed into camps the size of cities—walled in, denied basic freedoms, and left at the mercy of their oppressors.

Isn't it possible for both narratives to be true and valid? Yes, Jews were and are victims of racial hatred and anti-Semitism. And yes, Palestinians were and are victims of the emergence of a Jewish state through wars and occupation.

Dialogue ends when each side demands that the other "let go of past suffering" and "get over it." To ask a Jew to "get over" the systematic slaughter of 6 million fellow Jews is callous. To ask a Palestinian to "get over" his ejection from his family home and the forcible displacement of 700,000 fellow Palestinians is also callous. Both narratives of suffering and oppression are true. Both people have been and are victims.

Is it too much to hope that somehow Jews and Palestinians could weep together? Is it too much to hope that both acknowledge their own culpability? Is it too much to ask the church of Jesus Christ to play an honest and hopeful role in the devilishly difficult and complex challenge of peacemaking?

To that end it would be helpful to declare a moratorium on hateful speech and loaded terms: apartheid, racism, the treatment of Palestinians as "a new crucifixion," Palestinian activists and patriots as "terrorists." It would also be helpful if churches, of all places, made every effort to be balanced and fair, recognizing the legitimacy of both narratives and trying not to place blame on one side or the other.

As Christopher Leighton says in his article "False witness," we must resist both "the messianic zealotry that animates Jewish settlers" and the "anti-Zionist ideologues who have jettisoned the role of peacemakers because they believe that Palestinians cannot win unless Israelis lose."

A few years ago the Presbyterian Church (U.S.A.) said the church should "avoid taking broad stands that simplify a complex situation into a caricature of reality" in which one side is clearly at fault and the other side is clearly a victim. It's sound advice.

CAN WE TALK ABOUT ISRAEL?

May 16, 2014

For several years I met with a group of Christian and Jewish leaders to discuss the Middle East. Jewish participants were concerned that mainline Protestant churches seemed unbalanced in their attitudes about Israel. Christian participants wondered why Jews seemed consistently uncritical of Israel. After many intense and difficult conversations, we produced a statement. Two of the most significant understandings that we reached were:

—Not all criticism of Israel is anti-Semitic.
—Christians hope and expect more from Israel than from other countries because we value Israel's democracy, guarantees of civil liberties, and judicial processes. American Christians want Israel to thrive. We also expect more from Israel because of the substantial financial and military support that our nation provides.

I'm thinking about these statements as the Middle East peace process collapses in spite of Secretary of State John Kerry's herculean efforts. The *Chicago Tribune* and the *New York Times* proposed that the United States walk away from the situation and tell the Israelis and Palestinians to call us when they are ready to negotiate seriously.

Is there nothing hopeful and useful that the rest of us can do? Some support BDS—boycotts, divestment, and sanctions directed at Israel—although the only guaranteed result of that effort is the anger and alienation of the American Jewish community and damage to interfaith relations. As an alternative, I've long believed that financial investment in the Palestinian economy is a positive, practical, and hopeful gesture.

But here's a third option: it's time for mainline Protestant churches to invite mainstream Jewish organizations to sit down and start talking about what we can do together to support and animate the peace process.

Here's my argument: Israel needs to start acting as though it really believes a two-state solution is possible and the only solution that's viable in the long run. I have Jewish friends who agree. They do not approve of the settlements and understand that every expansion makes peace more difficult. I have Jewish friends who profoundly hope that the Israeli government will do what's necessary to bring about a sovereign, viable, and secure Palestinian state.

Writing in the *New York Times*, Thomas Friedman observes that two long-term trends make it extremely urgent to find a peaceful solution.[4] The first trend is the increasing influence of extremist forces within Israel that initiate violence and that refuse to consider an independent Palestine. An example of this is a recent attack on an Israeli military outpost by renegade Jewish settlers whom Friedman calls "terrorists." Another example, in the middle of the faltering peace talks, is the plan by Israeli housing minister Uri Ariel to build 700 new housing units in territory needed for a viable Palestinian state. Israeli justice minister Tzipi Livni commented, "Minister Ariel purposefully and intentionally did what he did to torpedo [the peace talks]."

The second trend is discontent among Palestinian youth. As Friedman says, the young generation of Palestinians "increasingly has no faith in their parents' negotiation with the Jews, [they] have no desire to recognize Israel as a 'Jewish state' and would rather demand the right to vote in a one-state solution."

American Christians and churches agonizing over the situation should consider reaching out to Jewish neighbors who are equally eager to find common ground: the end of settlement expansion, serious negotiation about compensation for Palestinian territory appropriated by Israel, and the status of Jerusalem as the capital of both states. Then together they could speak to American Jewish political lobbies that have influence with Israeli political leadership and to American Christian political lobbies that advocate for justice for the Palestinian people.

Friedman called John Kerry's relentless efforts to make peace "the Lord's work." Wouldn't it be something if Christian churches, hand-in-hand with Jewish neighbors, did the Lord's work of peacemaking?

DIVISIVE DIVESTMENT

July 7, 2014

At the 221st General Assembly of the Presbyterian Church (U.S.A.), held last month in Detroit, members of the governing body voted to allow Presbyterian clergy to preside at same-sex weddings in states where same-sex marriage is legal (see "PCUSA votes to divest funds, to marry gays where legal"). They also approved an amendment to the church's constitution that would change the definition of marriage from "between a man and a woman" to "between two persons, traditionally a man and a woman." For the next two years, 173 local presbyteries will debate and vote on the change.

This is a huge step toward full equality for the gay and lesbian community in the church and society.

The other issue that dominated the assembly was a vote to divest Presbyterian funds from three companies whose products are deemed harmful to the Palestinian people and prospects for peace: Caterpillar, Hewlett Packard, and Motorola. The economic impact on the corporations will be minimal; in fact, in an ironic twist, their executives may be relieved that Presbyterians won't be showing up at corporate headquarters asking for high-level meetings and offering stockholder resolutions. The vote has been noted by other mainline denominations agonizing over Israel's treatment of the Palestinian people and will be applauded by the international BDS movement (boycott, divestment, sanctions), whose supporters argue for abandoning the two-state solution—an independent and secure Palestine and Israel living together in peace—for a one-state solution in which Jews would be outnumbered and Israel, as a Jewish state, would eventually disappear.

The decision reverberated among those in the American-Jewish community, which overwhelmingly sees the move as anti-Israel if not anti-Semitic. Even Prime Minister Benjamin Netanyahu weighed in, sharply criticizing the Presbyterian decision on CNN.

Divestment did play a role in bringing down apartheid in South Africa and the government that enforced it. Yet I've never been comfortable with the analogy between South Africa and Israel. For one thing, South Africa made no pretense of being a democracy when it denied the vote and equal judicial process to the majority of its population. Israel at least has a constitution that guarantees rights to all its citizens.

Second, I've never been persuaded that divestment is effective. It has a seriously negative impact on interfaith relations; Presbyterian pastors and people are now scrambling to explain to Jewish friends and neighbors what the decision means and does not mean. Divestment also alienates a community of interfaith partners that have the potential to influence public opinion and Israeli policy.

Yet a third reason for my discomfort is the further division that we'll see within the Presbyterian family. I'm a veteran of Presbyterian struggles over race, gender, and sexual orientation, but this conflict seems to divide people more deeply than any other. Old and trusted friends are not only not listening to one another, they are barely speaking.

In the meantime the situation on the ground is messier than ever. Israel continues to make it difficult for its sympathizers by expanding settlements, overreacting to Palestinian violence, and torpedoing peace negotiations. The Palestinians struggle with attempts at unity between Fatah, a secular government in the West Bank, and Hamas, which governs Gaza. Hamas included a call for the destruction of Israel in its charter, continues to commit random acts of violence against Israel, and shows signs of moving toward an Islamist state.

The committee assigned to deal with the divestment issue was comprised of 50 or so randomly chosen commissioners or delegates. The national Presbyterian Church individuals who provided resources for the committee made no attempt at neutrality but advocated for divestment at every opportunity. So did hundreds of others inside and outside of the committee room, including representatives of Jewish Voice for Peace, a small but vocal group wearing green T-shirts with pastel stoles. Other demonstrators wore black T-shirts that announced, "Another Jew for Divestment," and young Presbyterians wore shirts that challenged observers to "Ask Me About My Trip to Israel/Palestine."

Committee leadership, which is supposed to remain neutral and ensure balance, did not do its job. At one point the vice moderator said, "Jesus was not afraid to criticize Jews. Why should we be?" My assessment is that the committee and the assembly were clearly leaning toward approving divestment.

When the committee's recommendation for approval came to the floor, Rabbi Rick Jacobs, president of the Union for Reform Judaism (the largest Jewish denomination), asked the assembly not to approve divestment. Jacobs declared his outspoken opposition to expanding settlements and Israeli intransigence and invited Presbyterians to partner with Jews to find a way toward peace and justice.

His plea did not change the decision. Now, in light of this development, Presbyterian leaders and people urgently need to reach out to Jewish neighbors. We need to explain that 49 percent of the commissioners voted against divestment and that it is the sense of many of us that a strong majority of Presbyterians do not agree with divestment and are distressed by it. We also need to explain that the church affirms Israel's right to exist, that it has made positive investments in both Israel and Palestine, and that it is committed to a two-state solution.

We also need conversations between supporters and opponents of divestment in the churches, with the goal of restoring civility and respect for one another and for Israelis and Palestinians, so that we can work together toward the elusive goal of peace with justice for which all of us so desperately yearn.

9
Culture
Wars

BUCHANAN PUTS his finger on an oft-repeated dynamic as liberals fight matters out with fundamentalists. The former keep trying to include the latter, who keep trying to exclude them. This dynamic plays out in the national political scene as well. Liberals believe in dialogue. Conservatives believe in principles and are convinced that anybody interested in dialogue has the implicit battle cry, "principles be damned!"

John's own battle cry (if we can call it that) is nothing so divisive. It is a claim that God's love is inclusive love, that Jesus is that love embodied among us. Therefore he'll talk to anybody: the protestor calling him a "baby killer," the neighbor who thinks his parents are going to hell, the historic enemies in faraway places. God has come near us in Christ. So we should not be afraid to come near to one another. The Baptist neighbors next door may have thought John's family was headed for the other place, but John has no problem writing them into heaven or giving his readers a glimpse of that beatific outcome as childhood neighbor Mr. Estep visits his ordination and takes some pride in helping get John there.

Over the past few generations in the United States, our culture has lurched to the left while our politics has lurched to the right. Gay marriage—often discussed in these pieces as a possible future—is now the law of the land. Abortion is not a lot less approved of than it was before the vociferous pro-life movement began. Yet our politics has been deluged with money from the far right, successfully questioning or stalling pieces of the welfare state, electing ever more unreasonably conservative candidates, wrapping itself in the flag as it makes life harder for poor people and easier for rich people. As these poles of politics and culture pull apart, what holds a people together?

The church used to be the center that holds. The Buchanans used to meet and befriend the Esteps. They were part of different churches, and they had their points of tension (the trumpets!), but they were neighbors and fellow Christians. Now our neighbors are just as likely to have no religion or a different one. More likely we have no idea what they believe or even what their names are.

If that's right, then dialogue, in the old-fashioned sense of just talking to one another, is a sensationally good idea. And if the mainline church can call for, exemplify, invite to, and even entice folks into a common life with neighbors that has largely been forgotten, we'll have done a great service in introducing a way beyond howling from the far right and left.

The culture wars may have done more to offer a counter-witness to the gospel than anything else in my lifetime. How can the church be God's agent for mending creation back together when we can't even mend ourselves? John Buchanan's witness as a church leader and editor of this journal has been to praise and model patience, dialogue, and mutual understanding. But what do you do when the other with whom you seek dialogue can understand himself only by denouncing you?

The troubling answer is: nobody knows.

CONVERSATION PARTNERS: EVEN IF WE DISAGREE

January 13, 2004

These are difficult times for people who value the unity of the church. The Network of Anglican Communion Dioceses and Parishes seems to be setting up as a rival structure to the Episcopal Church in preparation for a possible split of the denomination. In the Presbyterian Church (U.S.A.), the Presbyterian Lay Committee is proposing a "gracious separation." The dividing issue for Episcopalians and Presbyterians is the ordination of openly gay and lesbian persons, a step the Episcopalians took with the consecration of Bishop Gene Robinson. Presbyterians are forbidden to take that step with the offices of minister, elder and deacon by way of a constitutional provision added to the Book of Order in 1996. The Lutherans are currently talking about the issue and so are the United Methodists.

The issue of homosexuality has the potential to split these churches, not only because of the volatility of any question about sexuality and sexual practice, but also because there seems to be so little room to negotiate and compromise on this issue. Advocates of a more open and inclusive position and proponents of a more restrictive position both base their arguments on scripture and both claim the moral high ground.

In this context, it's good to have the example of Barbara Wheeler ("Strange Company: Why Liberals Need Conservatives") and Richard Mouw ("Hanging in There: Why Conservatives Need Liberals")—the example of Christians who profoundly disagree with each other on the issue of homosexuality but can talk with each other and stay in the same church together. Wheeler proposes a bracing image of the church as "tense, edgy, difficult—made up of strangers who cling to each other for dear life." After four decades of parish ministry and a decade or so of involvement with the national church as it has struggled with this issue, I like that ecclesiology a lot. And Mouw gets my attention, and moves me deeply, by calling all of us to lay our individual and collective sins at the foot of the cross.

One of the best resources for congregations struggling with this issue is *Homosexuality and Christian Community*, a collection of essays by members of the Princeton Theological Seminary faculty, who write from different points of view. These readable essays provide another model of how Christians who disagree with one another can still work, in the words of the Presbyterian ordination vows, to "further the peace, unity and purity of the church."

COUPLES: BRITNEY SPEARS'S ANNULMENT OFFERS A TWIST ON THE SANCTITY OF MARRIAGE

January 27, 2004

My morning reading the other day included four texts on sex and marriage that I carefully pondered: Dennis O'Brien's thoughtful essay, "A More Perfect Union"—which is published in this issue—expressing reservations about legalizing gay marriage; a *New York Times Magazine* analysis of the conflict in the Episcopal Diocese of Virginia resulting from Bishop Peter Lee's vote in favor of the consecration of Gene Robinson, an openly gay priest; a brave statement of conscience signed by 23 Roman Catholic priests in Chicago protesting the Vatican's condemnation of homosexual behavior; and, finally, a news item announcing that Britney Spears's 48-hour marriage had been annulled.

I suppose I elect to begin my day this way because I love the church, the whole church, belief in which I affirm every Sunday morning in the Apostles' Creed. I am vitally interested in church matters, and distressed when any part of the church is in trouble. In particular, I love the Presbyterian Church (U.S.A.) which continues its own struggles over homosexuality. I am also a pastor whose congregation includes people on all sides of this issue.

O'Brien patiently reasons his way through some of the complicated issues surrounding the legal recognition of gay marriages and civil unions, and he concludes that civil unions are preferable. I don't know whether I agree with him, but the article is strong, and it makes me think.

Bishop Lee's diocese includes leaders who are drawing a line in the sand between those who want a church broad enough to include a difference of conviction and biblical interpretation and those who regard truth as absolute and the tolerance of diversity as a bad postmodern idea. We are all going to have to argue over that one.

The Roman Catholic priests' statement moved me deeply, not only because I know and respect some of its signers, but also because it argues so eloquently that the "Catholic church is most catholic when it is inclusive and embracing, and least reflective of the Gospel of Jesus when it is exclusive and rigid."

The Britney Spears story came as an ironic twist on all of this. Those who argue for the sanctity of heterosexual marriage ought to be a little exercised about the actions of the wildly popular Ms. Spears. She and hometown friend Jason Alexander decided to get married after a weekend frolic in Las Vegas: "Let's do something wild, crazy. Let's go get married, just for the hell of it," Alexander said later, describing their attitude. That strikes me as an attitude more worthy of concern from those who care about the sanctity of marriage than the decision of a same-sex couple to live together faithfully and to love each other "in plenty and in want, in joy and in sorrow, in sickness and in health, as long as we both shall live."

GOD AND COUNTRY: WHY IS PLURALISM SO HARD?

January 10, 2006

Christmas 2005 may be remembered as the year arguments were revived over whether in the public square one should say "Merry Christmas" or "Happy Holidays." Target and Wal-Mart stores were boycotted by some evangelical Christians for their practice of referring to the "holiday." Some Christians even criticized President and Laura Bush for sending out a greeting card that said "With best wishes for a holiday season of hope and happiness." The card had no shepherds, angels, star or manger. And no Jesus. Some in the media charged that a "war on Christmas" was being prosecuted by secularists who want Christians to deny their faith.

Leonard Pitts observed in the *Chicago Tribune* that a deeper issue is involved: "An ever-more pluralistic society [is] struggling to balance the faith of the majority with the rights and feelings of the minority." He asked: "Why is pluralism so hard for these people?"[1]

The seasonal issue is also related to a fundamental political challenge: simultaneously allowing for the free expression of religion and avoiding the establishment of religion. Amy Frykholm's article ("Cadets for Christ") explores the way this challenge is being faced at the United States Air Force Academy. I am encouraged by Frykholm's report that the air force is at least trying to address the issue.

Experience leads me to believe that the Pentagon might benefit from the kind of reflection going on at the Air Force Academy. On a recent visit to the Pentagon with a group of clergy, I was taken to the very spot where the airplane struck on September 11, 2001. I was shown, through a window, the glide path of the plane as it approached the building. I noticed on that window sill a literature rack full of tracts with titles like "Where Will You Spend Eternity?" and "Jesus Christ Is the Only Way." My lunch companion was the chief of Pentagon chaplains, an American Baptist and a reader of this magazine. I asked him about the evangelical tracts—How did they get there? Are they legal?

The tracts are there, he said, because an evangelical group that focuses on reaching Pentagon staff puts them there. The building is public space, he said, and evangelical Christians are free to practice their religion in it. And then, gently chiding me, he added, "When's the last time mainline Protestants thought of doing something like that?"

That was one angle on the issue. A different angle emerged when the after-lunch speaker, a civilian Defense Department employee, got up and said, "I welcome you to the Pentagon in the name of our Lord and Savior Jesus Christ." I believe that the risen Christ is present in the Pentagon. But I confess that I was and am uneasy at hearing his name invoked in an official welcome.

MISLABELED: THE LIBERAL IMPULSE

October 7, 2008

Reflecting on the "disestablishment" of the mainline Protestant churches, Walter Brueggemann once observed that those churches and their members are for the time being living in a kind of exile. He offered the further challenging and comforting observation that though exile entails humiliation and suffering, it is not necessarily a bad place to be. In exile, God's people can say and do remarkable things.

One of the unhappy realities of living in exile is that one doesn't get to define the terms of public discourse. During the Republican National Convention I was recuperating from hip surgery, and I amused myself in front of the television by calculating how long it took for whatever speaker was at the podium to start bashing "liberals."

Labels are of limited usefulness, particularly when they are used pejoratively, but liberalism is an important thread in the fabric of our political history. The founders of the republic were Enlightenment thinkers, and in large part philosophically and theologically liberal. The liberal impulse in American politics is responsible for Social Security, Medicare and Medicaid, Head Start and food stamps. Liberals, often in face of fierce conservative opposition, have been the ones to guarantee equal rights, and they have made laws that help keep our food and automobiles safe and college education affordable.

In the theological arena, *liberal* has become such a negative term that few want to use it. *Progressive* has become the preferred alternative. There, too, conservatives have won the rhetorical battle.

I served briefly as an elected officer of my denomination and spent a lot of time trying to encourage dialogue between liberal and conservative factions. I observed that liberals don't like to fight, but instead are always trying to accommodate people, to be inclusive even of those who are trying to exclude them. And I concluded that the first thing on the minds of my conservative brothers and sisters when they get out of bed in the morning is fighting liberals, whereas liberals get out of bed trying to figure out how to live with conservatives.

The emergence of Governor Sarah Palin on the national scene has been accompanied by more rhetorical claims. The media have traced Palin's personal life (with her son who has Down syndrome and her pregnant, soon-to-be-married teenage daughter) as well as her policy stances (in favor of abstinence-only sex education and opposed to reproductive rights and to teaching evolution in public schools) to her Christian faith. I don't question Palin's faith; I simply hope that we can have a broader definition of the term *Christian* and acknowledge that some devout Christians believe in reproductive choice and more comprehensive sex education—not in spite of their faith but as an expression of it.

THE CASE FOR CONDOMS: BISHOPS VERSUS THE POPE

June 2, 2009

In March, when Pope Benedict XVI, on a flight to Cameroon, declared that the use of condoms is not the answer to the AIDS epidemic in Africa—that, on the contrary, it "increases the problem"—I thought immediately of Francis Ntowe. I met Ntowe years ago when he came to the U.S. from Cameroon. He became an elder in the Presbyterian Church. He cared deeply about the HIV/AIDS epidemic rampant in his native land and throughout Africa. (Of the 33 million people who live with HIV/AIDS, 22 million of them are in Africa, according to the World Health Organization.) Ntowe talked to anyone who would listen about the problem of AIDS in Africa.

One person who listened was another Presbyterian elder, Bernard Blaauw, a medical internist. Together with members of the Chicago church I serve, the two founded the Cameroon America AIDS Alliance (CAAA), which operates an AIDS clinic in Kumba, Cameroon, attached to a hospital operated by the country's Presbyterian Church. Blaauw heads up the clinic and is in residence in Kumba several months of the year. Members of my congregation support the clinic financially and volunteer at the clinic. Northwestern Memorial Hospital has donated equipment and furnishings worth more than $100,000.

In addition to treating patients living with HIV/AIDS, the clinic focuses on prevention. In a culture in which public discussion of sexuality and sexually transmitted diseases has been very difficult in the past and where condom use is low, the CAAA and Blaauw have conducted workshops for community leaders and pastors to equip them to speak openly about how AIDS is contracted and how it is prevented. There is a poster in the Presbyterian synod office in the city of Buea, Cameroon, that states the ABCs of AIDS prevention: A) Abstinence in the single life; B) Being faithful in married life; C) Condoms.

The pope is wrong about condoms. The overwhelming evidence provided by the World Health Organization and other health organizations is that proper condom use is the most effective way to prevent AIDS other than sexual abstinence. The Catholic Church's prohibition on artificial means of contraception has very little effect on the behavior of American Catholics. But its stance endangers millions of lives worldwide.

Blaauw was distressed by the pope's comment. He said that even though the mores of Cameroon discourage the use of condoms, they serve to save lives and prevent diseases and unwanted pregnancies. Blaauw said his clinic sells condoms for 22 cents. He would like to put out a bowl with free condoms in his office.

Despite the pope's statement, Roman Catholics are having a vigorous discussion on condoms. According to Catholics for Choice, Januário Torgal Ferreira, bishop of Portugal's armed forces, said, "I have no doubt that . . . prohibiting condoms is to consent to the death of many people." Bishop Manuel Clemente of Portugal commented that for people with HIV, condoms are "not only recommended, they can be ethically obligatory." Bishop Hans-Jochem Jaschke of Germany deplored the pope's comments and said, "Anyone who has AIDS and is sexually active . . . must protect others." Bishop Kevin Dowling of South Africa declared, "Abstinence before marriage and faithfulness in a marriage is beyond the realm of possibility here. The issue is to protect life." And in Cameroon, Cardinal Christian Wiyghan Tumi defended the use of condoms: "If a partner in a marriage is infected with HIV, the use of condoms makes sense."

I admire the courage of the bishops who speak out on this issue. And I am going to write a check to help Blaauw with that condom bowl in his office.

RHETORIC AND RAGE: WHAT IS AT STAKE

May 18, 2010

By all accounts, the crowd that gathered outside the temporary quarters of the Roman governor in Jerusalem on a Friday morning 2,000 years ago whipped itself, or was whipped by skilled political operatives, into an angry frenzy. The issue was what to do with a Galilean peasant who had run afoul of the carefully structured arrangement between the authorities of the occupied people and the greater authority of Rome, as represented by its appointed governor. The crowd became a mob that played a decisive role in the execution of a man innocent of wrongdoing.

Crowds can become dangerous mobs. The people in them can be swept up in anger and rage and may say and do things they would never do on their own.

Angry rhetoric on the public airwaves is also potentially dangerous. When a talk show host says, "We have to get rid of these people—these bastards," he crosses a line between expressing a political preference and inciting violence. Sure enough, violent and potentially violent acts began to happen to politicians involved in the health-care reform bill. Is there a connection between angry rhetoric and actual violence? Is there an accountability—if not legal, then at least ethical—that everyone who speaks publicly in a free society should be held to?

I believe that the rhetoric of rage is connected to violent behavior. Our fragile experiment in republican democracy, which is based on the God-given liberty of every individual, leans heavily on the tradition of civil dialogue—and that tradition fades in the midst of shouts and threats of violence.

Columnists and spokespersons from both sides of the political divide understand what is at stake. In the *New York Times*, Charles Blow cites a recent report from the Southern Poverty Law Center claiming that "nativist extremist groups have increased 80 percent since President Obama took office."[2] In the *Chicago Tribune*, John McCarron writes that "while Tea Party folks have some legitimate beefs . . . they better start guarding their right flank as well as their left. . . . Some unhinged believer will fly his Cessna into an IRS office in Texas, or blow up a federal building in Oklahoma City . . ."[3]

Wall Street Journal columnist Peggy Noonan says that there are many reasons why we have become a violent culture, but she says "one immediate thing can be done right now, and that is lower the temperature. Any way you can . . . . Just lower it."[4]

THE PATRIARCH NEXT DOOR: DEFINING FAITH

July 27, 2010

In this issue, Krista Tippett ("My Grandfather's Faith") recalls that as a teen she was eager to leave Oklahoma and a Southern Baptist grandfather who represented a "small, closed world defined by judgment."

According to him, "Every Catholic and Jew, every atheist in China and every northern Baptist in Chicago, for that matter—every non–Southern Baptist—[was] damned."

I wonder how many of us have a figure like that grandfather in our past—someone with a dominant personality whose strong faith, although it seemed confining, helped us define what our religion was and was not. For me that person is Mr. Estep, the patriarch of a family of ardent Baptists who lived next door when I was growing up. As there were only 20 feet between our houses, we could see into their kitchen and they could see into ours. In the days before air conditioning, we could pretty much hear everything that was happening in each other's houses—my parents in an occasional argument, Mr. and Mrs. Estep and their five children singing four-part harmony to "Blessed Assurance" with the mom at the piano. Occasionally the boys would bring out their trumpets, which irritated my father, who was sympathetic to their Christian fervor but believed that everybody should be quiet after dark.

Mr. Estep ran a tight ship: church on Sunday morning, Baptist Young People's Union followed by a Sunday evening song service with more trumpets, and Wednesday evening prayer service. He neither smoked nor drank alcohol, and his children, my chums, assured me that my parents, who did both, were in big trouble. The Esteps never went to a dance or a movie, never played cards or laid eyes on a Sunday newspaper. Occasionally I went to church with them in the evening. I excelled at Bible memorization and flirted with the girls (there were many more there than at my tiny Presbyterian Westminster Fellowship). My parents allowed me to go as long as I was with the Presbyterian tribe on Sunday mornings.

As I bridled at my neighbors' theological and eschatological exclusivism and came to understand the conflicts between their biblical literalism and what I was learning about the world, the Esteps and their religion defined for me what my religion was not. It occurs to me that my religion may have done the same thing for them.

Recently I've been thinking more about Mr. Estep. I remember that he taught me to throw a knuckleball and pitch quoits. I remember Mr. Estep and my father sitting on our patio on summer evenings talking, Dad smoking Camel after Camel, me listening to them talk until drowsiness drove me to bed. I recall Mr. Estep's interest in my attending divinity school (at an institution he wouldn't have touched with a ten-foot pole), his inquiries about my progress and his solemn handshake at my ordination—surely the only time he was ever inside a Presbyterian church—and his statement, "We're partly responsible for this, you know." Years later, when Mrs. Estep and my father were gone and my mother was very sick, Mr. Estep checked on her regularly, did her shopping and drove her to the doctor's office. He showed me what to aspire to in kindness and neighborliness. There's plenty of room in heaven for him—and for all of the Esteps, so long as they don't get out their trumpets after dark.

ALTERNATIVE WAYS

August 4, 2011

In 1997 I traveled to Croatia on behalf of my denomination to visit the Reformed churches and the Evangelical Theological Seminary in Osijek. The shooting war had stopped, but bullet holes marked the facade of the hotel I stayed in. Racial and religious hatred was palpable. We talked with Roman Catholics who blamed the Serbian Orthodox for the violence and with Orthodox who blamed the Catholics and Bosnian Muslims. During my stay Presbyterian mission worker Steven Kurtz drove me across a bridge. As soon as we passed the Croatian checkpoint he removed his clerical collar and shoved it under the front seat. "What are you doing?" I asked. "That collar gets me through the Croatian checkpoint, no questions asked," he said, "but it could get me shot, or detained for a long time, on the other side."

In his book *Exclusion and Embrace,* Miroslav Volf writes out of his experience of life in Croatia. In the preface, he reports how theologian Jürgen Moltmann once asked him if he could embrace a Chetnik, one of the Serbian fighters who had been burning churches and raping and killing in Volf's native land. Volf answered: "No, I cannot—but as a follower of Christ I think I should be able to."

Volf is one of the few major theologians read by both mainliners and evangelicals. He taught at Fuller Seminary and is now at Yale Divinity School. In this issue ("All due respect"), he reflects on a verse in 1 Peter, which he says speaks to Christians' relations with non-Christians. Volf insists that the text means what it says: honor everyone, even the one you do not agree with, even the one you believe is utterly wrong.

How we relate to the "other," ethnically, nationally, religiously, is the most important moral and theological issue of our time. It is so easy to identify all Israeli Jews with fanatical settlers, all Muslims with suicide bombers. It is easy for outsiders to identify all Christians with the radical fundamentalists who threaten to blow up abortion clinics.

Shirley Guthrie, in *Always Being Reformed,* writes that the results of Christian exclusivist thinking are always the same. "First, those who are sure their interpretation of the gospel is the correct one try to 'help' others understand and accept their true religion. . . . If that does not work, then in one form or another, violent or nonviolent, come the crusades, inquisitions, religious wars, and colonial or economic or cultural imperialism that try to *force* everyone to accept and live by this or that version of true Christianity."

Is there no alternative to the dreary dynamic of "my way is the only way, and the only way you and I will ever be reconciled and live in peace is for you to acknowledge the error of your ways and believe what I believe and become what I am"?

There is an alternative. We can view religious diversity as part of God's economy. We can hold together two ideas: that God's love is universal and unconditional, and that Jesus Christ is the full expression of that love.

LIFE AND HEALTH

February 21, 2012

I recall three times when the churches I served were picketed. On one occasion, some neighbors were opposed to a development project in which the church was a partner. The opponents handed flyers to worshipers as they arrived and departed, describing what they claimed would be the disastrous repercussions of the proposal. The picketers wore large round badges with the image of the new building, including the church at its base, crossed out with a big red X.

The second incident cut more deeply. Some Presbyterian officials on a study trip to the Middle East met with and said positive things about representatives of Hezbollah and Hamas. This was in the midst of church proposals to divest from corporations whose business in

Israel was deemed harmful to the Palestinians. Representatives of the Jewish community picketed on a Sunday morning to express unhappiness with the Presbyterian Church (U.S.A.). Fortunately, the church had a strong relationship with a local synagogue and with major Jewish organizations. In a way, the Sunday morning picketers underscored the importance of the relationship and actually spurred more meaningful dialogue and shared mission activity with our Jewish neighbors.

The third incident, and by far the most traumatic, had to do with abortion. For some time the church I served in Ohio had been providing start-up office space for a religion-based organization that advocated for reproductive choice. After an intense discussion, the church Session had allowed the use of the space. An influential voice on the Session, I recall, was that of a distinguished, generally conservative woman who said firmly that a woman's body was her own business and responsibility.

A group opposed to legal abortion showed up on several Sunday mornings to carry placards in front of the church. I went out to meet them, introduced myself and invited them in for a conversation. The discussion went badly. In fact, it wasn't a conversation at all. I asked for the opportunity to explain why the church did what it did and was met with a barrage of harsh rhetoric and accusations.

On my last Sunday as pastor of the church, the protesters returned with large placards bearing bloody images of fetuses and signs that read: "Buchanan Is a Baby Killer" and "Good Riddance."

I was reminded of those confrontations as I followed the controversy over the decision by Susan G. Komen for the Cure to cut funding for breast exams at Planned Parenthood clinics—and over its subsequent decision to restore its funding of Planned Parenthood. Since some Planned Parenthood clinics perform abortions and provide information on abortion, it has become a favored target of anti-abortion groups.

At the heart of the controversy is the fact that Americans are conflicted on the issue of abortion. A great many individuals are conflicted within themselves.

I object to the monopolization of the term *pro-life* by groups whose agenda is to make abortion illegal and deny women the right and responsibility to decide this very personal matter. I am certainly not "antilife," nor am I proabortion. I am for choice. The issue is whether women should have that freedom.

Since 1973 that decision has been a guaranteed right, and I think that, given the moral ambiguities that surround abortion, it is a right that makes sense.

I know from experience that positions on this issue are deeply held. But I continue to think that we can be civil in our disagreement and that we ought to look for common ground where we can—such as on supporting women's health.

SAME OLD SLANDER

July 22, 2013

In this world of constant change, one thing remains absolutely predictable: the *Wall Street Journal* will never miss an opportunity to bash mainline Protestant churches. The paper has regularly printed harsh critiques of progressive churches and ecumenical organizations. Particularly mean-spirited have been its attacks on the World Council of Churches and the National Council of Churches—full of half truths and innuendo, forcing clergy to explain to their congregations what those organizations actually are and do. The newspaper's editors seem to find particular joy in the challenges facing Episcopalians and Presbyterians.

Why this consistent, persistent hostility? Is it because progressive churches have kept alive the truth that the gospel of Jesus Christ has social, economic and political implications that often challenge the profound individualism of the *Journal*? Is it that followers of Jesus Christ, in gratitude for their individual salvation, often get together in these churches with other followers to try to make the world a little more reflective of the biblical view of peace and justice?

Many theological conservatives have now embraced mainline Protestants' concern for gender equality, for protecting the environment and for reducing the widening gap between rich and poor. Evangelical preachers are now reminding people that Jesus talked a lot more about poverty than he did about sex. Evangelical churches are now including issues of peace and justice in their mission. But not the *Wall Street Journal*. Instead, the paper continues to repeat the same old worn-out complaints.

So it is that a *Journal* book review (July 5) turns into yet another attack.[5] To review Elesha J. Coffman's book *The Christian Century and the Rise of the Protestant Mainline* (reviewed in the May 9 *Century* by David Hollinger), the *Journal* called on Barton Swaim. Coffman's thesis is that the *Christian Century* was a voice, conscience and unifying force for mainline denominations in the early and mid-20th century.

In Swaim's account of mainline history, Harry Emerson Fosdick is referred to simply as "the anti-fundamentalist preacher," as if that is all Fosdick ever was. Swaim is particularly harsh and unfair to Charles Clayton Morrison, the *Century*'s founder and editor from 1908 to his retirement in 1948. Swaim refers to Morrison's "characteristic pomposity" and somehow finds offensive Morrison's goal of influencing the "best minds in the church" in hopes that "they will in turn influence the laity." How that goal is pompous eludes me. It sounds like a pretty good idea—in fact, it sounds like a definition of theological education.

Swaim dismisses outright what he calls mainline Protestant leaders' "high-flown argumentation about social justice and political positions that were unpopular, manifestly ridiculous, or both." He illustrates this claim by citing Morrison's and the *Century*'s support for Prohibition—a cause backed by almost all Protestant leaders of the early 20th century.

Swaim reveals his real intent when he chides Coffman for "treating her subject too delicately, with a young scholar's reluctance to draw broad conclusions. So allow me."

The rest of Swaim's essay rehashes the old line that the mainline churches are declining numerically because their leaders embraced unpopular and radical positions. Does he mean positions in favor of racial equality or in favor of dialogue with communist China? Does Swaim have in mind the concern for stewarding God's good creation? Does he believe that these issues are not morally and theologically important? Or is it that these positions have collided with adamant individualism and conservative politics?

The low point of the review is when Swaim accuses the *Century* editors—and Martin E. Marty in particular—of "dirty tricks" in pursuing their criticism of Billy Graham in the 1950s. Coffman reports merely that the editors were suspicious of Graham's finances and tried to investigate them.

Swaim ends by unloading on mainline church leaders for denying the authority of scripture and telling people that one cannot know that God exists. He either doesn't know or prefers to ignore the traditional theological conversation about what it means to "know" God: we cannot know God exists in the same way that we know a table and chair exist. The best theologians through the ages have reminded us that God is not an object to be observed in the same way we observe other objects. Rather, God is the source and ground of existence.

The numerical decline of the mainline churches is a complex topic, which deserves serious study and discussion. Swaim says nothing new or helpful. But then, as he tells us, that was never his intent.

10
The Reading
Christian

A REGULAR READER of the *Century* complained to me once that "it seems like all they care about is Palestine, movies, and the Democratic Party." As he ticked off the triumvirate, I found myself counting how many times I'd written about each of the three! This section of John's pieces on reading shows the unfairness of the critique. John recommends a dizzying array of books. Sure, there's a center of gravity in his recommendations: theology, church life, politics, history, fiction. But there are also suggestions far outside the expected field. It's anything but narrow.

I sometimes think this is the most important thing the *Century* publishes—John's regular, giddy announcement of the treasures he's found between book covers that he delights to share with others. He's showing the delight of the pastoral office: it's one of reading and writing, one where God shows up between the pages and the people's lives—ours' included. Many academic friends of mine don't actually read. They'll put a book on a syllabus just to make themselves read it (some let down from one-time dreams about "the life of the mind"). Buchanan uses Joseph Sittler here to illustrate why pastors often don't read: there just isn't time. John doesn't just rebuke us, scolding, "Well, then, you should *make* time."

He shows us his pleasure in making time and the way that time has been rewarded in more fruitful ministry in the church.

Some books here we really have to drag ourselves into reading, such as whatever our parishioners are reading, however inclined we are to ignore it, university-trained snobs that we are. Most reading is a treat, however. John offers a range of reading options in hopes that lots of us readers will find something that delights us too. C. S. Lewis imagines friendship being born in that moment where we say, "Wait, you too? I thought I was the only one!" No wonder so many readers regard John not just as a writer but also as a friend.

A ninety-five-year-old parishioner said to me once, "When you're ninety-five, you know you don't have a *lot* of time left." He went on to say, "My main regret is that there are so many books I haven't read yet." Buchanan reports the same sadness here, passed on from Martin Marty. Yet we have the hope of Jorge Luis Borges, who says he's always imagined heaven as a sort of library. If so, we won't run out of time to read or time to talk about what we're reading with others, the way the Buchanans once modeled for their son John. And maybe that's *how* these are the most important pieces in the *Century*. The final pieces in this book point to the end of all things: a raucous library, full of learning and discussing books, maybe even, as James Howell has daringly suggested, spending time with "fictional" characters who populate our imaginations. Fantastic? Surely. But John's delight hints at an even greater delight when God will be all in all.

READ ALL ABOUT IT: SUMMER READING

October 11, 2000

Though neither of my parents had a college education, I learned from them the joy of reading. Our home was one in which the Sunday *New York Times* was divided and carefully passed back and forth, and the crossword puzzle was a shared project. Winston Churchill's books on the Second World War were on the bookshelf, and so were Carl Sandburg's volumes on Abraham Lincoln.

My parents loved not only to read but to talk about what they were reading. When I was assigned Ole Edvart Rölvaag's *Giants in the Earth* in high school, my mother procured a library copy so we could discuss it. When my college sent out a recommended reading list to incoming freshmen, she ordered all the books and insisted that I take a volume to work on my summer job for the Altoona Water and Sewer Department. I recall having a copy of George Orwell's *Animal Farm* tucked in my back pocket and trying to explain to my fellow workers what it was about.

So I became a reader. Here are some of the books I put in my suitcase this summer—and I'm glad I did:

Adam Cohen and Elizabeth Taylor's biography of Richard J. Daley, *American Pharaoh*, is must reading for students of American urban politics and, of course, all Chicagoans. Jack Rogers's *Reading the Bible and the Confessions* was enormously helpful to this Presbyterian who hopes and prays for the day his church will be more inclusive. Rogers traces the way the church has changed its mind about what the Bible means by what it says in regard to race, slavery, divorce, remarriage, and the role of women.

A good friend gave me a copy of Philip Yancey's *What's So Amazing About Grace* and said, "You're going to like this." She was right. Yancey is such a good writer and such a generous evangelical that even though I occasionally disagree with his conclusions, I'm glad to be in the same family with him.

Another book that was on my list this past summer was Miroslav Volf's *Exclusion and Embrace*, a thoughtful and provocative exploration of some of the most vexing theological, political and social dilemmas of our age.

I also loved being reintroduced to St. Augustine by Garry Wills's new, accessible biography, and especially encountering Augustine's insight that "since it is God we are speaking of, you do not understand. If you could understand, it would not be God." And Wills includes this delightful observation by Augustine, made near the end of his life when the doctrine of the incarnation was reshaping his views about human physicality: "Man's maker was made man that He, ruler of the stars, might nurse at His mother's breast."

STOCKING THE SHELVES

September 12, 2001

At the end of summer my mother would launch her annual canning process. She retrieved large Ball jars from the cellar, sterilized them in boiling water and sealed tomatoes, beans and rhubarb from Dad's garden into them. The food would appear on our dinner table throughout the winter.

I follow that tradition, modestly, by making strawberry and blueberry jam every year, but even more by storing away information and ideas gleaned from my summer beach reading. With no less care than mother gave to putting up food I plan ahead, carefully choosing my books. My hope always is to store away substantial, lively homiletical material that will help me through a winter of preaching.

This year I reread Gary Dorrien's two-part essay on postliberal theology, which we published in our July 4–11 and 18–25 issues.[1] Instead of trying to make Christian faith reasonable, says Dorrien, the church should concentrate on making it visible. George Lindbeck put it like this: "Pagan converts to the early church did not absorb Christian teaching intellectually and then decide to become Christians. They were attracted to what they saw of the faith and practices of early Christian communities." Sounds like a faithful growth strategy to me.

Huston Smith's *Why Religion Matters: The Fate of the Human Spirit in an Age of Disbelief* was alternately stimulating, irritating and provocative. Frederick Buechner, in *The Eyes of the Heart*, shared eloquent and moving descriptions of experiences common to us all.

Roger Angell's *A Pitcher's Story: Innings with David Cone* reinforced my passion for baseball. The son-in-law of the late E. B. White, Angell is better than anyone else at describing the mysteries and particularities of the national pastime.

Ghost Soldiers, Hampton Sides's gripping account of the 1945 rescue by U.S. Army Rangers of 513 survivors of the Bataan Death March, was a moving reminder of human sacrifice, resiliency and hope. I loved Richard Lischer's *Open Secrets: A Spiritual Journey Through a Country Church*. Like Lischer's, my theological education was refined and completed by a small congregation of extraordinary Christians and unforgettable characters who initiated me into—and somehow survived—my early and confident attempts at ministry.

Finally, I appreciated *John Adams*, David McCullough's biography of the man who shaped, participated in and wrote about the formation of our system of republican democracy. It is also about his equally extraordinary wife, Abigail, who wrote him, "In the new code of laws . . . I desire you would remember the ladies, and be more favorable to them. . . . Do not put such unlimited power into the hands of husbands." Much of this book will, as they say, preach.

BOOKISH: READING AND THE PASTORAL VOCATION

October 9, 2002

I grew up with books. My parents valued books and taught me to treat books with respect and affection. One of the unexpected pleasures of college was going to the bookstore to purchase the texts I needed and could afford, and carrying them back to my room—my own books. I still have some of them. And I still love the feel of a newly purchased book in my hands.

In divinity school I got the idea that part of the pastoral vocation is to read—to keep up with what the biblical scholars and theologians are saying, and to stay in touch with the culture by reading novels, biographies, histories, journals, magazines and newspapers. I recall an anecdote from one of Joseph Sittler's lectures, which he later included in a 1959 *Century* essay, "The Maceration of the Minister." It was a poignant portrait of the overworked, hassled minister who had been determined to sustain a discipline of lifelong scholarship, but whose desk was cluttered not with open texts but with a set of blueprints for the new education wing and a sample of linoleum floor tile.

I've tried to keep faith with Sittler's hopes for us and I read as much as I can. I was delighted to discover in a recent survey that 25 percent of *Century* readers have purchased ten to 14 books in the past 12 months, and 35 percent have purchased more than 14.

I was further pleased to learn that the *Century* plays a supportive role in our subscribers' reading lives: 65 percent said they had purchased a book because of a *Christian Century* advertisement, and 71 percent have purchased a book based on one of our reviews.

When we asked our readers what types of books they had purchased in the past 12 months, we learned that "theology" was far and away the most popular category, with 75 percent checking this box. Other top interests (in order): spirituality, fiction, history, biography and pastoral care. I find all of that encouraging.

My wife and I were browsing recently in an art shop in Wilmington, North Carolina, that specializes in ceramic pop art. We found a few pieces we liked. I bought a square ceramic plaque with the primitive figures of two children and overhead the bold, red inscription, "READ BOOKS." I do. And so do most of you.

NOVEL IDEA: GOOD NOVELS CAN NOURISH THE WORK OF PREACHING

May 31, 2003

I am mostly a utilitarian reader. For 40 years I have been writing and preaching sermons weekly, and I have come to rely on the almost exact relationship between the quality and quantity of my reading and my ability to create a sermon that has some life and energy to it. Good reading—of Bible commentaries, books on theology and culture, essays, journals—stimulates whatever it is in me that produces sermons.

What I don't read enough of are novels—books that don't immediately commend themselves as aids in sermon writing. As a New Year's resolution I determined to read a few books just for the pleasure of reading. It has been great fun, and I have found that these books do nourish the work of preaching.

I can commend Louis Begley's *About Schmidt* and Jonathan Franzen's *The Corrections*. Begley's short novel was rewritten for the film version. I loved the book, which is about profound loneliness and our capacity to hurt those people we most deeply cherish. And I couldn't put Franzen's novel down. It's about a midwestern American family, and I felt as if I knew personally each of its amazing characters.

The Spooky Art: Some Thoughts on Writing, by Norman Mailer, is not a novel, but it is outrageous, funny, irreverent and beautifully crafted. I learned more than I wanted to know about the trials and tribulations of trying to earn a living by marketing one's art. And I confirmed a growing sense, suggested by Mailer's *The Gospel According to the Son*, that there is a spirituality here, mostly unnamed and unclaimed by the author.

The unlikeliest and in many ways best of the novels I encountered is *Balzac and the Little Chinese Seamstress*, by Dai Sijic. The author was born in China in 1954 and was "reeducated" during the cultural revolution of the 1970s. The book is about two boys who are sent from the city to a rural village for reeducation—their convoluted and sometimes hilarious life working as laborers, their friendship with a seamstress and their theft of a suitcase full of forbidden material (classic French novels in Chinese translation). It's a wonderful story about the way art liberates the human spirit.

John Updike has chronicled and critiqued American life more than any other writer, and I savored his 20th novel, *Seek My Face*, which presents a daylong conversation between a 78-year-old painter—the widow of a Jackson Pollock–like figure—and a New York interviewer. I learned a lot about postwar American art, and found myself rereading Updike's exquisite descriptions. Updike, by the way, takes faith seriously, has read and understands Karl Barth, and actually goes to church.

A DOOR TO THE INTELLECT AND HEART

October 19, 2004

This issue's emphasis on books exemplifies one of the things I have most liked about the *Christian Century* over the years: it has helped me to decide what books to purchase and read. I'm still relying on it to do that. For example, I'd like to read all eight recommendations in the field of New Testament.

I'm reminded of my first investment in books. As a student pastor I was spectacularly unprepared to be a minister and to preach. A friend sent me to the old Pilgrim Press bookstore in Chicago; I found it in the Loop, climbed the stairs and explained my plight to the kind woman behind the counter. "I have $100 to spend and need some books to help me get started being a minister."

She didn't blink, and better yet she didn't laugh out loud. She led me to the Bible section and pointed to an impressive set of encyclopedia-like volumes. She explained that *The Interpreter's Bible* contained both exegetical material and commentary, and she suggested that I purchase the volumes on the four Gospels, Romans and Exodus. I had money left over for the Book of Common Worship and two volumes of sermons. Her final gift to me was to refuse my money. Because I was a student, she said, I could have the books on account and pay for them when and how I was able.

I discovered shortly thereafter that my academic mentors didn't think highly of *The Interpreter's Bible*, but those volumes helped me for a while. They remain on my shelf as a kind of monument to that kind bookstore clerk and also to my initiation into a lifelong concern for connecting believing and thinking—which, for me, happens in the act of reading.

I believe more than ever that reading opens a door to the intellect and heart that visual forms such as television simply miss. I am sick to death of the political attack ads on television, which use every visual trick in the book to create a negative image. I snap off the television in disgust, wondering what these slick ads have to do with the incredibly important decision the American people have to make.

Writing can be manipulative too, of course, but the act of reading generally involves critical faculties in a way that the viewing of images does not. Jeffrey McCall, a DePauw University professor of communication, recently commented in the *Chicago Tribune* about how to assess the televised presidential debates.[2] He observed that "presidential elections are too important to turn on a consultant-designed one-liner." McCall's advice? Don't watch the debate. Read about it in the newspaper the next day.

A GREAT CALLING: GRATITUDE FOR
AN AMAZING VOCATION

April 19, 2005

One of my laments over the years has been over the dreadful image of clergy in popular media. With some notable exceptions, ministers are portrayed as inept, shallow, out of touch with the world and basically irrelevant—like Chaplain Mulcahy in the old *M*A*S*H* television series. Clergy occasionally show up in novels, like John Updike's *Month of Sundays*, for instance, but even Updike, who writes about serious theological and moral matters, has laypeople, not clergy, doing the heavy lifting.

So it was a delight to read during Lent three books which feature lively, somewhat eccentric and altogether human clergy: Marilynn Robinson's *Gilead*, Tony Hendra's *Father Joe* and Anne Lamott's *Plan B: Further Thoughts on Faith.*

John Ames, the 76-year-old narrator of the novel *Gilead*, is one of my favorite characters. He is the pastor of a small congregation in Gilead, Iowa. His father and grandfather both served churches before him and are fascinating characters as well. His grandfather was an austere, zealous abolitionist who came to Kansas to participate in the Civil War, "preached men into war" and entered the pulpit in a bloody shirt and with a sidearm at the ready. His son, another John Ames, became a pacifist, partly as a reaction to his father's zeal.

The narrator of *Gilead* is painfully aware of his mortality. His heart is failing, although his emotion and spirit are profoundly alive. Ames is thinking about the day in the not-too-distant future when he will be gone and his congregation will find a new minister and perhaps undo many of the traditions and structures that characterize his ministry. Who among us clergy hasn't thought like that?

I was struck repeatedly with the accuracy of Robinson's description of what it feels like to be a minister. Ames says that writing is like praying, that in interpreting scripture and writing sermons the minister is engaging in an act of personal devotion. Ames speaks movingly about the privilege of baptizing infants, about "that feeling of a baby's brow against the palm of your hand," and about how it is always a source of truth and wonder to hold the baby and see the expression of affection and deep emotion on the faces of parents.

Ames loves his life and his ministry, and is not particularly happy about giving them up. He knows that "when you do this sort of work, it seems to be Sunday all the time." He is unhappy about the influence of radio preachers, whose certainty about heaven and hell eliminate the mystery from faith. When he thinks about dying and St. Paul's promise that "we shall all be changed in the twinkling of an eye," he thinks it will be like "going for a line drive when you are so young your body almost doesn't know about effort." And heaven must be "your child self finding me and jumping into my arms."[3]

Passages like those—and there are plenty of them—stopped me in my tracks and renewed my gratitude for this amazing vocation.

WRITERS AND WORDS: SPRING READING

March 10, 2009

When unusually balmy weather occurs after a season of cold and snow, some of us cannot resist thinking about baseball. As I write, pitchers and catchers are packing up for their spring training—an event that for baseball fans is like the first Sunday in Advent for Christians. Like sap rising in the spring, hope again rises in our hearts.

Baseball inspires devotion and great writing. One of my favorite books on the subject is the collection *Diamonds Are Forever: Artists and Writers on Baseball.* Among other remarkable essays, it contains John Updike's "Hub Fans Bid Kid Adieu," about Boston Red Sox slugger Ted Williams's last game. (In Updike's title, which mimics the sports page headlines, "Hub" refers to Boston; "Kid" was Williams's nickname.)

Updike, who died in January, and whom I have been quoting for several issues,[4] describes Fenway Park, the fans and the home run that Williams hit with his final swing. It's the stuff of sport mythology, and Updike was up to recording it. He tells of how Williams was running around the bases "at the center of our beseeching screaming . . . as he always ran out home runs—unhurriedly, unsmilingly, head down, as if our praise were a storm of rain to get out of." The crowd continued to cheer after Williams entered the Red Sox dugout, pleading with him to return to the field for a tip of his hat. Updike's words may be the best ever written about that moment in baseball: "Our noise for some seconds passed beyond excitement into a kind of immense, open anguish, a wailing lament to be saved. But immortality is nontransferable. . . . Gods do not answer letters."

I never met Updike, but I'm still grieving his death because he has been a stimulus to my thinking, a resource throughout my ministry. His death reminded me of two other authors who died recently and who also had provocative things to say about religion and God. Norman Mailer was a colorful character who seemed to love the roughest and seamiest side of life. Not long before he died he granted a series of interviews, which are published in the book *On God*. Mailer said that he was an atheist for 30 years before coming to acknowledge that he did believe in God. He tried reading theology and was repelled. Theologians, Mailer concluded, "were undernourished in their appetite for inquiry." I wish he could have had a conversation with the theologian Joseph Sittler, for one. Mailer came to believe in God, he said, because of his intense lifelong "exploration of human reality." He envisioned God as "an artist, not a lawgiver, a mighty source of creative energy," and human beings as God's "most developed artwork."

Novelist Kurt Vonnegut, who died two years ago, referred to himself as an "unbelieving believer." The author of *Slaughterhouse-Five* once said that perhaps the most important words anybody ever uttered are "blessed are the meek." Not long before his death, Vonnegut said: "If I should ever die, God forbid, let this be my epitaph: The only proof he needed for the existence of God was music."

ST. ERNEST?

April 17, 2012

I've been reading a lot about Ernest Hemingway lately, and my interest extends to the other expatriate writers living in Paris in the 1920s, such as Gertrude Stein and F. Scott Fitzgerald. I've long believed that Hemingway's late novel *The Old Man and the Sea* should be required reading for anyone who presumes to speak publicly because of its economy of prose—crisp, lean sentences that use no unnecessary words. So I thoroughly enjoyed Woody Allen's film *Midnight in Paris,* which is about a modern would-be writer who travels in time back to Paris in the 1920s. Actor Corey Stoll nicely captures Hemingway's belligerent, confrontational manner and displays his literary style: "The bread is good and strong and true!"

I recently read Paul Hendrickson's *Hemingway's Boat: Everything He Loved in Life, and Lost, 1934–1961,* which focuses on Hemingway's love of the ocean and of boating, fishing and entertaining in Key West, Bimini and Havana before the Castro revolution. Hendrickson describes the boat, *Pilar,* as well as the company that designed and built it, the caliber of its engines and the quality of its amenities, giving those of us who aren't sailors more information than we need.

He also mentions several of Hemingway's friends who are not covered extensively in other biographies and shares his far-reaching interviews with Hemingway's sons. The man who emerges is a study in contrasts. He was an impossible boor. He drank too much. He alienated friends, humiliated people who wanted to be near him and emotionally and verbally abused his wives. But he was also capable of graciousness and generosity, as in his relationship with his youngest son, Gigi, a physician who was a cross-dresser for most of his life and died in a Miami jail for women. He once wrote to friends grieving for the loss of their 15-year-old son: "We must live it, now, a day at a time and be very careful not to hurt each other."

Author Reynolds Price proposed that Hemingway yearned for "sanctity." I'm not sure what to make of that unusual comment, but Hemingway's persistent yearning is clear. In his novel *Across the River and into the Trees,* a character seems to be speaking for Hemingway when he says: "Why am I always a bastard? . . . [Why can I not] be a kind and good man? . . . God help me not to be bad."

After spending years immersed in Hemingway's work and life, Hendrickson appears to agree with Price. He offers this poignant conclusion: "I have come to believe deeply that Ernest Hemingway, however unpostmodern it may sound, was on a lifelong quest for sainthood, and not just literary sainthood, and that at nearly every turn, he defeated himself."

A PASTOR'S STUDY

March 12, 2014

One of the best essays I've ever read on the practice of ministry is Joseph Sittler's "The Maceration of the Minister."[5] Sittler reflects on how the seminary student is solemnly told that big concepts like the kingdom of God (*basileia tou theou*) demand a lifetime of study and reflection. But then the student becomes a pastor. Sittler's description of the transition still makes me laugh out loud:

> Visit the [former student] years later in what he inexactly calls the "study" and one is more than likely to find . . . a roll of blueprints; a file of negotiations between the parish, the bank and the Board of Missions; samples of asphalt tile, a plumber's estimate.

The pithy paragraph came to mind almost every day of my final year of ministry because our congregation was moving through a major building project. I even had my own hard hat with my name on it, and I'd look at it sitting on my bookshelf and ruefully remember Sittler's words.

Many of us love the busyness, energy, and creative dynamism of a robust church. Many of us love the program direction and even the management. And yet all of us pastors must summon an uncommon discipline if we are to reflect the priority and importance of preaching.

It can be done. Sittler wrote:

> It [the congregation] is likely to accept, support and be deeply molded by the understanding of Office and calling which is projected by its minister's actual behavior. It will come to assess as central what he, in his actual performance of ministry and use of his time, makes central.

The preacher, Sittler concluded, must order her or his time around study, reflection, and sermon preparation. I discovered that the congregation appreciates knowing that the minister takes preaching seriously. The practice I developed—and it's not unique or original—was to block off segments of time throughout the week for reading, study, and sermon preparation and to be strict about never infringing on them. I learned the hard way that sermons not grounded in a significant investment of time were not very good.

At first I felt guilty about affording myself the luxury of uninterrupted time. But I came to understand that this was what the church's members called me to do, were willing to pay me to do. I told the personnel committee and church leaders about the time I devoted to preparing sermons and was delighted to have their understanding and support of my attempt to honor those who invest a morning of their busy lives in coming to church and listening to what the preacher says, always hopeful that it will contain a word from the Lord.

SHELF SPACE

October 7, 2014

I once had the privilege of presiding at the wedding of a seminary president and a professor of homiletics. I said in the homily that I wasn't concerned about the longtime viability of their relationship, but I was worried about how they would manage to combine their personal libraries.

I'd like to claim that idea as my own, but it was inspired by Anne Fadiman's essay "Marrying Libraries," in her book *Ex Libris: Confessions of a Common Reader*.

Fadiman wrote that it was good that the Book of Common Prayer didn't say anything in the marriage vows about marrying libraries and throwing out duplicates. "That would have been a far more solemn vow, one that probably would have caused the wedding to grind to a mortifying halt."

I reread that essay recently when my wife and I moved, and it became apparent that the time had come to weed out books from my library. I knew that day would come, but I dreaded it. I love books. I love owning them. I like to hold them in my hands. When I visit other people's homes, I cannot keep my eyes off the books they are reading. I like to see what my seatmate on the plane or the woman sitting across from me on the bus is reading. I keep books for work in one place and books read for pleasure in another. I have a special place for big books of art, photography, and travel and always several books on my bedside table.

Now it was time to decide which books I could live without. I looked at each title on a shelf, sometimes opening it to see what I had underlined or written in the margins. Inevitably I decided I couldn't part with it. An hour of scanning books usually resulted in a paltry two or three volumes to be given away. I kept at it, becoming more ruthless with each pass. Finally I had a number of boxes ready to be taken away. But I still had most of my books.

The ones I kept included Bonhoeffer's *The Cost of Discipleship*, the reading and rereading of which taught me that faith is far more than intellectual assent. I've kept half a shelf for works by Kathleen Norris and Barbara Brown Taylor. Frederick Buechner, Harvey Cox, and William Placher easily made the cut. Martin Marty's entire shelf remains, and it felt downright insensitive and irresponsible to consider letting go of Joseph Sittler's few small volumes. I kept Gustav Aulén, Karl Barth, and Paul Tillich—even though I never made it past page 50 of Tillich's *Systematic Theology*.

I may have at it again sometime—but I doubt it. I have committed myself at least to keeping a state of equilibrium: every new book must occasion an old book's departure. What will be done with all the books that remain? It's a problem that I really don't mind leaving to my children and grandchildren to resolve.

Afterword

Serving as editor/publisher of the *Christian Century* from 1999 until 2016 was one of the nicest things that ever happened to me. In many ways it was a dream job. For one thing, heading up a journal like the *Christian Century* isn't hard work. Journalists are introspective self-starters. They come to work in the morning, sit down at their desks, sometimes close the office door, and go to work in solitary splendor. They occasionally emerge for a cup of coffee or to ask someone a question. But for the most part they neither require, nor want, supervision.

In addition, the *Christian Century* has maintained, over many years, the highest professional journalistic standards. People who work for the magazine are very good at what they do, and they do it because they believe deeply in what the *Christian Century* aspires to be: a resource for thoughtful people of faith who think critically about all things, including religion; who are committed to engaging faith and culture, politics, economics; and who want to be part of the ongoing theological conversation about the intersection of religion and the world at large. In 1999 I joined a staff of deeply committed, highly skilled journalists led by Associate Editor David Heim, who knew how to produce a thoughtful journal every week or so. It was a staff happy to be working together. Simply being part of the rhythm of the *Christian Century* was a great gift to me and something else I had not anticipated: a valuable resource in my own ongoing vocation as a pastor of a congregation and a preacher. And I had new friends, smart, erudite, eloquent friends, committed to values that are central to me. What could be better than that? So I here wish to express my gratitude to each one of them.

The Board of Trustees that oversees the work of the magazine and to which I have been accountable has been an additional valuable resource, offering wise counsel and careful financial oversight. At a time when print publishing all over the world is fragile with declining subscriptions and advertising, the *Christian Century* is stable financially. With Peter Marty's fresh leadership as publisher and the addition of younger staff who live comfortably in the brave, new, digital world, the future of the magazine remains hopeful and promising.

The editorials in this book reflect not only my own thinking but what was happening in the world, nation, and church during the past seventeen tumultuous years. They begin with the tragic death of John F. Kennedy Jr., son of President John F. Kennedy, an event that, for me, marked the end of an era, my formative era. It was the high hope of Kennedy's New Frontier and his stirring inaugural, "Ask not what your country can do for you. Ask what you can do for your country," that resonated deeply and suggested that a life of public service could be a sacred calling. When I first experienced the Christian faith and the Christian church as players in American culture and resources for building a better, kinder, more peaceful, and more just society, my own call to ministry became clear. The civil rights movement was the context. Kennedy was initially slow to understand the power of the demand for equal justice that was emerging in the late 1950s and early '60s, but he did finally lead in a way that resulted in the Voting Rights and Civil Rights Acts under his successor, President Lyndon Johnson.

It is a sobering reality for me that as I write my nation is reeling following a series of police killing African American men, the murder of five Dallas police officers by a black man intent on killing white people, and a newly energized and determined Black Lives Matter movement. It seems as if we are more divided racially than ever. And yet, out of the tragedy and grief of the moment there is emerging a new understanding of institutional racism, the ways that racism is deeply embedded in American culture, how that plays out in our common life, and also a renewed gratitude for law enforcement and the danger faced every day by the men and women who serve in our police departments. The shooting in Dallas that resulted in the deaths of five policemen occurred while police were accompanying and protecting a Black Lives Matter protest rally and march. Significantly the police were not wearing the military-style gear, body armor, and helmets that we are accustomed to seeing at events like this, but short-sleeved uniform shirts, an eloquent reminder that protest is not an act of war but a fundamental right of all Americans. There were even pictures of police officers chatting with protesters and posing for selfies. The absence of riot gear obviously increased the vulnerability of the police, but I continue to see hope in that reminder of our common humanity, that all of us desperately want a society that is just and safe for everyone.

It reminded me that eight years ago the American people did the unthinkable: we elected an African American man to be our president. Four years ago we did it again. It reminded me that part of the vocation of people of faith is to find light in the darkness. We have, in fact, come a long way in terms of racial justice, and we have a long way yet to go toward the goal of liberty and justice for all. People who understand the centrality of justice in our faith must continue to advocate, argue, pray, and work for that good and sacred goal in the days ahead.

Looking back over the past seventeen years, I confess to chagrin and disappointment that efforts to regulate the sale and ownership of firearms, even in minimal, common sense ways, continues to be difficult. The NRA and its supporters in Congress have been hugely successful in arguing that the Second Amendment right to bear arms in order to raise a "well-regulated militia" actually means that a person deemed a threat to the community by law enforcement agencies still has the right to purchase, and in some states carry openly in public, a military semi-automatic rifle designed not for target practice but to kill as many human beings as quickly and efficiently as possible. The utter insanity of that has been demonstrated over and over again in an unprecedented series of mass killings in elementary schools, high school cafeterias, movie theaters, and office parties, and still the braying about the unrestricted right to bear arms continues. In addition, the NRA and its minions have successfully convinced millions of Americans that there is a conspiracy to take away their guns and that every reasonable effort at gun control is evidence of that conspiracy, which, of course, is fabricated nonsense. We are awash in guns that continue to kill innocent people. There is plenty of unfinished business for people of faith in the days ahead.

2016 is an election year, and the nation is in the midst of one of the most unusual, negative, and divisive presidential campaigns in recent memory. Sometime in the past several decades, the traditional conservative and liberal/progressive divide in American politics deepened, due in part to the emergence of a radical right wing symbolized by the Tea Party. That movement now dominates the Republican Party. Moderate Republican voices have been silenced and moderate candidates defeated in primary elections. The result is a profound ideological fissure in the body politic that has made compromise impossible and governing very difficult. After the 2008 election, the Republican majority leader of the U.S. Senate declared that his one overriding priority in the days ahead would be not to assure that Congress finds a way to govern by working with the new administration but to assure that Barack Obama is not reelected. Martin Marty and others have labeled it the "new tribalism," and regardless of who wins the current presidential election, it will be with us for the foreseeable future.

The Republican presidential candidate, Donald Trump, although singularly uninterested in value issues such as abortion and gay marriage, nevertheless has tapped into the tribalism of the Republican right wing with promises to build a wall along the border with Mexico, restrict immigration, target all Muslims for official suspicion, and return the nation to a time of mythological greatness. Evidence of the power of the ideological divide is that Christian evangelical leaders, who ordinarily would be appalled at the candidate's personal lifestyle and marital history, recently endorsed his candidacy, one of them asking fellow evangelicals to cut him some slack because he is a "baby Christian."

The moderately progressive tradition in American Christianity, represented by the mainline Protestant denominations, has its work cut out for it in the days ahead. American culture desperately needs a religious presence and voice that is reasonable, that thinks carefully and critically, that is free of fundamentalism and captivity to ideology, that is hospitable and welcoming and as inclusive and gracious as Jesus himself was. It is, in my mind, absolutely imperative that the voice of reasonable, progressive, intellectually rigorous and open Christianity be maintained.

It will be a challenge because the mainline churches continue to decline, both in membership and influence. It's not the Episcopal Presiding Bishop or the Presbyterian Stated Clerk who are quoted in the media but Franklin Graham and James Dobson. Financial constraints, following membership loss, have resulted in reduction in denominational staffs and mission commitments. As numbers of members, congregations, and dollars continue to decline, it is apparent that something huge is happening. The foundation of the mainline Protestant establishment is crumbling. Looking back at the long history of the people of God, one scholar called the phenomenon an "every-five-hundred-year rummage sale" during which old, worn items are discarded to make room for the new, at the end of which the institution itself is renewed and stronger.[1] Others see what is happening as a new reformation. Something is dying and something is struggling to be born, and no one knows what exactly is coming next for the church. It reflects even larger shifts and changes in the culture itself. Robert P. Jones, CEO of the Public Religion Research Institute's new book, *The End of White Christian America*, documents the shifting religious and ethnic population of the United States.

Still the denominations survive and house the great ecclesiastical and theological traditions. Executive and mission persons continue to do good and faithful work. In communities and neighborhoods all across the country, mainline congregations serve the poor, welcome the outcast, proclaim Good News, and convey, in their very presence, hope and kindness, peace and justice.

The future will require innovative and creative leadership that remembers and retains the best of the Protestant tradition, particularly the fact that the tradition was born five hundred years ago in the midst of a protest against an established institution. That has implications for the way theological education and preparation for ministry and church leadership happen. It has implications for the way we go about being a church faithful to Jesus Christ in a culture where we no longer dominate. I find myself thinking a lot about something my pastor said directly to me in the Charge to the new pastor at my ordination. It was prescient, and it is still a good and important Charge for the church and for all of us who continue to love it. "John," he said, "you are not called to be successful. You are called to be faithful."

I remain hopeful. I refuse not to be. More and more I find myself pondering that long historical trajectory of the people of God and the sense that a good and compassionate and just and loving Holy Other is always a presence, deeply involved in whatever is happening, however difficult and painful. Looking at the relatively brief trajectory of American history and the role of the people of God in it, I am hopeful about prospects for both the church and the nation. How can I not be?

> Do not remember the former things,
>   or consider the things of old.
> I am about to do a new thing;
>   now it springs forth, do you not perceive it?

Isaiah 43:18–19

Notes

Introduction

1. Harold Fey, "Seventy Years of the Century," *Christian Century*, October 11, 1978, 950–54.
2. "The Christian Century," Wikipedia, https://en.wikipedia.org/wiki/The_Christian_Century.
3. See Martin E. Marty, *The Protestant Voices for American Pluralism*, George H. Shriver Lecture Series in Religion in American History (Athens: University of Georgia Press, 2004).
4. See Phyllis Tickle, *The Great Emergence: How Christianity Is Changing and Why* (Grand Rapids: Baker Books, 2012).

Chapter 1: The Mainline and the World

1. This column was among the first pieces John Buchanan wrote for the magazine after assuming responsibility as editor and publisher. At the time, people were wondering whether the magazine should change its name to reflect the start of a new century.
2. Ralph C. Wood, "Rest Not in Peace," *Christian Century*, February 3, 1999, http://www.christiancentury.org/article/2012-02/rest-not-peace.
3. Hans Kung, *Christianity: Essence, History, Future* (New York: Continuum, 1996).
4. "No-Fault Division?," *Christianity Today*, July 1, 2004, http://www.christianitytoday.com/ct/2004/july/22.23.html.
5. Russell D. Moore, "Where Have All the Presbyterians Gone? Nondenominational Churches Are the Fastest Growing in the Country," *Wall Street Journal*, February 4, 2011, http://www.wsj.com/articles/SB10001424052748703437304576120690548462776.

Chapter 2: Ministry and Church Life

1. Ian Frazier, "Hungry Minds: Tales from a Chelsea Soup Kitchen," *The New Yorker*, May 26, 2008, http://www.newyorker.com/magazine/2008/05/26/hungry-minds.

2. Peter Steinfels, "On Things Religious: Written and Unwritten," *The New York Times*, January 2, 2010, http://www.nytimes.com/2010/01/02/us/02beliefs.html?_r=0.

Chapter 3: In the News

1. This was John Buchanan's first "Editor's Desk" column written post-9/11. The September 12 issue of the *Century* was already at press when the events of that Tuesday morning unfolded. The September 26 issue contained a word penned by the editors jointly, "What Does God Intend?," http://www.christiancentury.org/article/2001-09/what-does-god-intend.

2. David Kennedy, "Fighting an Elusive Enemy," *New York Times*, September 16, 2001, http://www.nytimes.com/2001/09/16/opinion/fighting-an-elusive-enemy.html.

3. Elisabeth Rosenthal, "Where Did Global Warming Go?" *The New York Times,* October 15, 2011, http://www.nytimes.com/2011/10/16/sunday-review/whatever-happened-to-global-warming.html.

Chapter 4: War and Peace

1. Peter Steinke, "Fear Factor: Psalm 27:1–14," *Christian Century*, February 20, 2007, http://www.christiancentury.org/article/2007-02/fear-factor.

Chapter 5: Matters of Faith

1. Fareed Zakaria, "A Guest of My Time: 'The Kennan Diaries' by George F. Kennan," *The New York Times*, February 21, 2014, http://www.nytimes.com/2014/02/23/books/review/the-kennan-diaries-by-george-f-kennan.html.

Chapter 6: Popular Culture

1. David Kirkpatrick, "In 12th Book in Best-Selling Series, Jesus Returns," *The New York Times* (March 29, 2004), http://www.nytimes.com/2004/03/29/us/in-12th-book-of-best-selling-series-jesus-returns.html.

2. Jason Byassee, "Be Happy: The Health and Wealth Gospel," *Christian Century*, July 12, 2005, http://christiancentury.org/article/2005-07/be-happy.

Chapter 7: Civic Engagement

1. Katharine Moon, "The Sins of the Preachers," *Chicago Tribune*, March 25, 2008.

2. David Rothkopf, "20 Things That Won't Survive the Crisis," *Foreign Policy*, February 19, 2009, http://foreignpolicy.com/2009/02/19/20-things-that-wont-survive-the-crisis/.

3. "Long Legs of the Crash: 13 Unexpected Consequences of the Financial Crisis," *Foreign Policy*, January 10, 2009, http://foreignpolicy.com/2009/10/01 /the-long-legs-of-the-crash-13-unexpected-consequences-of-the-financial -crisis/.

4. Rahm Emanuel, "Emanuel on Occupy: Listen to the Anguish," *Chicago Tribune*, October 14, 2011, http://articles.chicagotribune.com/2011-10-14 /opinion/ct-perspec-1014-emanuel-20111014_1_anguish-mayor-rahm -emanuel-middle-class.

Chapter 8: The Middle East

1. Roger Cohen, "Jews in a Whisper," *New York Times*, August 20, 2011, http://www.nytimes.com/2011/08/21/opinion/sunday/cohen-jews-in-a-whisper .html?pagewanted=print&_r=0.

2. Edmund Sanders, "Glenn Beck's Israel Tour Raises Eyebrows," *Los Angeles Times*, August 23, 2011, http://articles.latimes.com/2011/aug/23/world /la-fg-israel-beck-20110823.

3. Jonathan Rosen, "A Missionary Impulse: 'The Crisis of Zionism' by Peter Beinart," April 15, 2012, http://www.nytimes.com/2012/04/15/books/review /the-crisis-of-zionism-by-peter-beinart.html.

4. Thomas Friedman, "Not the Same Old, Same Old," *New York Times*, April 16, 2014, http://www.nytimes.com/2014/04/16/opinion/not-the-same-old -same-old.html.

Chapter 9: Culture Wars

1. Leonard Pitts, "The Season of Forbidden Good Cheer," *Chicago Tribune*, December 13, 2005, http://articles.chicagotribune.com/2005-12-13 /news/0512130249_1_merry-christmas-christmas-tree-christian.

2. Charles M. Blow, "Whose Country Is It?" *New York Times*, March 26, 2010, http://www.nytimes.com/2010/03/27/opinion/27blow.html?_r=0.

3. John McCarron, "When a High-Minded Movement Is Ambushed," *Chicago Tribune*, April 12, 2010, http://articles.chicagotribune.com/2010-04 -12/opinion/ct-oped-0412-mccarron-20100412_1_tea-party-minded -protesters.

4. Peggy Noonan, "The Heat Is On: We May Get Burned," *Wall Street Journal*, March 27, 2010, http://www.wsj.com/articles/SB10001424052748704094 104575144070064980374.

5. Barton Swaim, "Behind the Decline: The Magazine That Fueled Liberal Protestantism's Brief Ascendancy in American Culture," *Wall Street Journal*, July 5, 2013. http://www.wsj.com/articles/SB10001424127887324328204578569253573107528.

Chapter 10: The Reading Christian

1. Gary Dorrien, "A Third Way in Theology: The Origins of Postliberalism," *Christian Century*, July 4, 2001, http://www.christiancentury.org /article/%252Fthird-way-theology and "Truth Claims: The Future of Postliberal Theology," *Christian Century*, July 18, 2001, http://www.christiancentury.org /article/2001-07/truth-claims.

2. Jeffrey M. McCall, "Voter's Guide to Watching the Presidential Debates," *Chicago Tribune*, September 29, 2004, http://articles.chicagotribune.com/2004 -09-29/news/0409290136_1_presidential-debates-candidates-one-liner.

3. Marilynne Robinson, *Gilead: A Novel* (New York: Picador, 2004).

4. See also "The Glory of the Mundane: Remembering John Updike" in the February 24, 2009, issue and "Bookshelf Riches: Recommended Reading" in the February 10, 2009, issue.

5. Joseph Sittler, "The Maceration of a Minister," in *The Ecology of Faith: The New Situation in Preaching* (Minneapolis: Fortress, 1961).

Afterword

1. Phyllis Tickle, *The Great Emergence: How Christianity Is Changing and Why* (Grand Rapids: Baker Books, 2008), chap. 1.